ES-CAPE OF GEN-ER-AL Mc-CUL-LOCH.   *Frontispiece.*

HISTORY OF OHIO

IN WORDS OF ONE SYLLABLE

BY

ANNIE COLE CADY

AUTHOR OF "HISTORY OF NEW ENGLAND," "HISTORY OF PENNSYLVANIA," ETC.

WITH ILLUSTRATIONS

APPLEWOOD BOOKS
BEDFORD, MASSACHUSETTS

History of Ohio was first published in 1888 by Belford, Clarke & CO.

Thank you for purchasing an Applewood Book.
Applewood reprints America's lively classics—
books from the past that are still of interest
to modern readers. For a free copy of our
current catalog, write to:
Applewood Books
P.O. Box 365
Bedford, MA 01730

ISBN 1-55709-554-X

Library of Congress Card Number: 00-110666

PREFACE.

In sending forth this unpretending record of
Ohio's struggles and triumphs from her birth to
the present time, I have sought to make it both in-
structive and interesting to the little people for whom
it is written, and with this end in view have left out
many dates and dry details of events which would
be considered indispensable in a more advanced
History.

Special thanks are due to Celia Logan, Colonel
Donn Piatt, Dudley Selden Nye, postmaster of
Marietta, and some others for valuable information
given, and assistance in the work.

Owing to the limitations of the book, I have been forced to leave out some events, and also many people's names whose careers entitle them to the esteem and love of the rising generation. So it is with a feeling of regret that I lay aside my pen, realizing how far I have fallen short in my efforts to do justice to this noble State.

A. C. C.

NEW YORK, *September* 20, 1888.

CONTENTS.

LIST OF ILLUSTRATIONS.

HISTORY OF OHIO.

CHAPTER I.

THE RED MEN.

As this great ball which we call the earth speeds on its course through space, men come and go on its crust, and whole tribes pass off and are known no more.

In our own fair State this change has gone on for —who can say how long a space of time? We have no book which tells us of the men who lived on the banks of our bright streams ere La Salle, the first white man, came.

But we know men did live here, for we have the great mounds which they made, and the forts they used to keep off some foe of which we may not have heard.

What these great mounds were made for we are not quite sure; but the wise men who make such things the thought of their lives tell us they think the mounds were made to put the dead of some tribe in. To prove this they have had a few of these dug o-pen, and high piles of bones which once made the frames of men were found.

Most of these bones were so old, that when they were brought to the light and air they soon turned to dust. A few of the large ones kept their shape, and have been put in glass cas-es for us to see if we like.

Who lived here be-fore these mound-build-ers, as they are called, we do not know; but this is an old, old world, and we are ver-y young.

In the ground of this fair State, bones which do not go to make up man are found. Bones which tell us that once the el-e-phant roamed through our woods and drank from our streams; and bones, too, which tell us of a larg-er beast still, the great mas-to-don, by whose side the el-e-phant was both small and weak.

Would you not like to have lived in those days just for a few hours, so that you could take a peep at those strange, wild things who looked at this land all a-bout us as their own?

It seems strange, does it not, that there are men so wise that they can tell from one or two bones which they find, all a-bout the be-ing of which they once formed part. Those men have told us a great deal of this land, and the strange things which once lived here, of which we with-out their aid could not have guessed.

MOUND AT MAR-I-ET-TA.

Men have tried and are still try-ing to find out more of the men who built the mounds. Now it is thought they were Red men.

The great rings of earth which are found near the mounds, and are called forts by the white men who now live near them, were made to raise the land on which their homes were to be built, so they could see a foe while still a long way off. There are few hills in this part of the State ; hence the Red men made them where they liked.

If we trust to these wise men still more, we learn that on the tops of each of these rings of earth, a long, slim house once stood. This house, which was the home of the whole tribe, was made of wood, and cut up in-to small square rooms.

It is thought that, like the Red men of the North and West, the food for a great tribe

IN-DIAN PIPES.

was cooked at one place, in a great pot, or by the

side of one great fire. If their meal was of broth, the girls and wom-en of the tribe formed a line, and with bowl in hand marched to the pot, took their share, and made their way back to their homes in the " long house," where, it must be guessed, they all ate from the same bowl.

How they slept, or what they did when not on the hunt or war path, we do not know. They must have worn fur rugs wrapped a-bout them, in the cold months at least ; and small holes in the top of the long house must have been left to let out the smoke of the fires they built on the floors of their homes to keep Jack Frost at bay. Thus they lived on their plain lives, and did not dream that a race would one day come who should change their wild land to one filled with great cit-ies, and crossed and re-crossed by a net-work of wires and rails which bring the thoughts and men from the ends of the world to their doors.

CHAPTER II.

THE FIRST WHITE MAN.

At one time a French man named La Salle, lived far north in Can-a-da. He saw much of the

LA BELLE RI-VI-ERE.

Red men of these parts, as he bought their fur skins and the fish they were glad to sell for his gold or guns.

He learned to talk with these men, and must have been well liked by them. When their trade was done, we are led to think they were prone to stop and chat with the white man, as men of to-day are at times known to do. How else could he have learned of the fair land to the South, or the bright stream he made up his mind to see?

In the fall of 1669, La Salle, with some Red men as guides, pad-dled up the St. Law-rence to Ni-ag-a-ra, where he crossed to our side. With the aid of his guides, he made his way as best he could down the streams, or o-ver the land, with his bark boat, till he reached the Al-le-gha-ny; and when here it did not take him long to float down to the stream the Red men called Ō-yo, the riv-er he had come so far to see. So fair and bright it seemed to this lone man, as he saw it for the first time, framed with its high banks and tall trees, that he gave it the sweet name of *La Belle Riviere*—"the beau-ti-ful riv-er,"—by which it was known for a long time.

He sailed on down its breast, proud and glad that no white man had looked on these rich scenes be-fore, till his way was barred by the falls where Lou-is-ville now stands. Here he turned and made his way

back by the same route he came, and did not then
know that the wa-ter on which he had sailed so long,
in time made its way to the Gulf of Mex-i-co, but
thought the riv-er flowed on to-wards the west till
at last its wa-ters joined those of the great Pa-cif-ic.
Men in those days thought the Pa-cif-ic but two or
three hun-dred miles to the west.

La Salle was so much pleased with the land
through which he passed, and the " La Belle
Riviere" he had found, that he wished as the
months went by that he knew more of the land
through which the fair stream flowed, and where at
last it met the sea. Twice in vain he tried to do
this; but a third time he start-ed, and in A-pril, 1682,
reached the Miss-is-sip-pi. He was full of joy, as
day by day on his voy-age down he saw new charms
in the land through which he passed. In time he
reached the mouth of the stream, and was the first
man to write of this tract through which he had
sailed.

He named all the land drained by the Miss-is-
sip-pi and its branch-es, *Lou-is-i-an-a*, for the King of
France, Lou-is IV. For fear lest the Eng-lish should
claim this whole land, the French king had a chain
of forts built all the way from Can-a-da to the Gulf.

Now the Eng-lish claimed not on-ly all this
" North-west Ter-ri-to-ry" as it was called, but all the

land west of the coast line which the two Cab-ots
sailed up in 1497 and 1498. Then at one time the
Red men gave to Eng-land all the land drained by
the O-hi-o Riv-er, in a trea-ty or kind of deed.

You know New Eng-land was filled with men
from Old Eng-land, who from time to time sent
a-cross the sea for char-ters which told them just how
far each col-o-ny should reach. Now the king had
no i-de-a how large this land was. He could tell from
the maps which were brought to him the shape and
size of that strip which stretched a-long the coast, and
he knew that off to the west was a great sea called
the Pa-cif-ic. So he would draw his lines at the
north and south of the land he was to bound, with
great care; and then in a free sort of way would add,
" from the At-lan-tic to the Pa-cif-ic." Thus Mass-
a-chu-setts in these old char-ters reached to the Pa-
cif-ic, and Con-nec-ti-cut did the same.

No one thought there was much land far west
from the Hud-son, till La Salle found the O-hi-o,—
then Eng-land was quick to claim it as her own. So
you see it was not safe for French or Eng-lish to try
to make homes there, for they would be sure to
be sent off by the oth-er side. So for long years the
Red men lived on in their old, wild way af-ter the
tribes on the coast had been killed off, or sent far
back in the woods by the white men.

A few French, friends of these tribes, lived near or with them, and trad-ed French guns for their skins

IN-DIAN TRAD-ER.

and game. In this way all the tribes soon learned to use fire arms.

The first O-hi-o Land Com-pa-ny was formed in Vir-gin-ia in 1748. This sent a man named Chris-to-pher Gist to find a spot on which to build a trad-ing post. In 1750, Gist reached the Eng-lish trad-ing post of Pick-a-wil-la-ny, which was the first point set-tled by the Eng-lish in O-hi-o. It was built in the year 1749, by men from Penn-syl-va-nia, but in 1752 the French; with the Red men near by, burned the fort, killed four-teen men, and took the rest to Can-a-da ; and thus came to an end the first fort made by the Eng-lish.

All this time the French did what they could to keep friends with the Red men. They went so far as to take the young squaws for wives, and at times lived in wigwams, just as the Red men did.

In the spring of 1649, the French king sent some plates made of lead to be placed in the ground of such parts of this land as was claimed by them. On each of these plates he wrote that the land on which it was found was his, and warned all men of that fact. A long time af-ter this, in 1798, two boys jumped from a high bank in-to the Musk-ing-um for a swim ; while in the wa-ter one spied a strange shaped stone—as he thought it to be—in the bank near by. He climbed to the spot, and with the help of his friend drew a large lead plate from the soil. " Just the thing for bul-lets," thought the boys; and they cut great chunks from its edge to melt for them, ere it was known by their friends that such a plate had been found. At first there was some doubt as to who placed it there in the earth ; but when a man who could read French saw it, he told them how it came to be there. The boys made no more shot from it ; and in 1821, Ca-leb At-wa-ter sent it to Gov-er-nor De Witt Clin-ton, who in turn gave it to a club of wise men in Bos-ton, who take pride in just such strange things. It can be seen in their rooms to-day if you care to go there to look at it.

CHAPTER III.

FRENCH AND INDIAN WAR.

THE men in Penn-syl-va-nia, as well as those in Vir-gin-ia, wished to have pow-er in the land now known as O-hi-o. The soil was rich, the woods fine, and the streams well filled with fish ; while game was to be found in all parts of the land. In 1744, some men in Penn-syl-va-nia bought a tract of land on the O-hi-o, of the Red men ; but for some cause they did not get a full ti-tle to this for eight years. At last, in 1752, they made new terms with the Red men, and built a fort at the forks of the O-hi-o. But the French still held the land, and with the help of the Red men killed all the Eng-lish who went far from the banks of the riv-er. These French had forts in all parts of the land ; they had built some, and still held all those which the king had built years be-fore.

At last Gov-er-nor Din-wid-die, of Vir-gin-ia, sent Ma-jor George Wash-ing-ton, then but twen-ty-one years of age, to St. Pi-erre, the French Chief at Fort Le Bœuf, four hun-dred miles a-way.

Wash-ing-ton went in the cold fall and winter storms, through the woods where no paths were to be found, and gave the word he had brought to the Chief. But the French would not

HOW THE FRENCH MAN'S WIFE CAUGHT FISH.

stop their sad work, or give up one jot of their claim ; and said they would fight if need be to hold it. So Wash-ing-ton's long ride did no good.

In March, 1754, the O-hi-o Com-pa-ny built a fort where Pitts-burgh now stands. Thir-ty-six men were at work on it, but ere it was done, a large force of French and In-dians float-ed down the stream, and took the fort for the French.   They called it Fort Du-quesne.

AN IN-DIAN AT-TACK.

This might be called the first act of the " French and In-dian War," which for nine long years filled our land with woe.   From this wild fight in the woods of O-hi-o, the war spread to all parts of the world, so that ere it was done, all the lands in the known world might be said to have tak-en part. In all parts the Eng-lish won.

In Feb-ru-a-ry, 1763, peace was made at Par-is. By the terms then made the French gave up all their land in A-mer-i-ca, east of the Miss-is-sip-pi, but a small spot near New Or-leans.

Though this was at an end in all the rest of the world, the In-dians near the O-hi-o did not care to have it so. They liked to fight, and had been taught by the French to hate the Eng-lish, so paid no heed to the "Trea-ty of Par-is."

The Red men were ruled o-ver at this time by Pon-ti-ac, as great a chief as ev-er lived; and he formed a plan by which he hoped to kill all the Eng-lish on the land drained by the O-hi-o Riv-er.

In the spring of 1763, bands of In-dians came down up-on each of the Eng-lish forts which were placed on the edge of this land. Two hun-dred men were killed, and nine of these forts fell in-to the hand of the foe. De-troit, which was then a part of what was known as O-hi-o, was watched for months; but would not give in. Men came to help those in some of the forts, so that Pon-ti-ac did not do what he thought he should. It was a sad time for the folk who lived near our land; and fear was felt by some that we should not know in this spot, at least, what the word peace meant. But the men in those days were brave, and did not give up when once they had made up their minds to do a thing ; and we have to thank them for the firm way in which they worked to rid our land of a foe which would ev-er stir up war and strife.

CHAPTER IV.

PONTIAC.

ONE who knew this chief, and the tribes o-ver which he held sway, tells us way back in 1765, that he was more like a king than a chief. His men were to be found in all parts of the North-west, and he had full pow-er in the land. He lived in as fine style as he knew how to.

In 1670, Ma-jor Rog-ers was sent with a strong force of men to whip some French who had not kept their word, and were at war with our men in the North. As he came to the land which was held by the great chief, Red men were sent to him to tell him that their chief was not far off, and wished him to stop where he then was, that Pon-ti-ac might come and see him with his own eyes. When they met,

Rog-ers told the In-dian why he had come, and went on to say that the French were as much foes to the In-dians as to the Eng-lish. The In-dian king seemed pleased with the ma-jor, and wished him to stay a short time in his town. While the troops were there, the In-dians did all in their pow-er to

IN-DIAN CA-NOE.

make them at ease, and when they went on their way, Pon-ti-ac helped them in all ways he could. He was much pleased with their sad-dles, and wished to know just how their clothes were made, and how they wore them. He tried to learn all he could of the white man's mode of war, and seemed to wish to be more like them in all ways. He said that he would be pleased to own the King of Eng-land, not as a *king*, but as an *un-cle*, as of course he would not give up his own pow-er ; but that he would show his

kind will to the far-off un-cle by gifts of furs and the
like. He would be glad to grant fa-vors to the Eng-
lish in this coun-try, and would let them come and
live in what part of his land they chose, if they would
but own him king of the place. If they would not

IN-DIAN HOME.

take his terms, he "would shut up the way and keep
them out." Hence from the last war, of which you
have just read,—that of 1763, which is known as
"Pon-ti-ac's War,"—we are led to think that the
Eng-lish did not do as he wished.

While De-troit was in such a sad plight, a large band of men were on their way, in the south of the land, to burn the In-dian towns on the Mus-king-um. But ere they reached the first of these they were met by more than fif-ty chiefs who sued for peace. At last Col-o-nel Bou-quet, who was at the head of the Eng-lish, said he would spare their homes if they would give up all the men, wom-en, and chil-dren they had taken from us in the long war which had just passed. The chiefs thought for a while, and at last said they would give up all near at hand in twelve days, but those far off in the North could not get here till spring. The cold months were then up-on them, and they could not bear the long tramp through the cold and deep snows they would meet on the way. The Red men did as they said they would ; and it was a bright day for the white men when they saw once more the dear faces of wives and children they thought must have long since died at the hands of the foe.

This act of the In-dians made friends of all, and there was no more war in our land for ten long years.

CHAPTER V.

LORD DUNMORE'S WAR.

Aт this time there were bad white men in O-hi-o
who liked to do mean deeds quite as well as some of
the low men of to-day do ; and these men did all the
bad things they could think of to the In-dians.   At
last, with no cause for the act, they killed all the
friends and kin of the great chief, Logan, so that it
was said he had not a child or dear one left in the
world.   This was a wick-ed act, and all our men had
to suf-fer for the sins of those few bad ones.   Lo-gan
was the strong chief of the great Min-go tribe, all
of whom were now foes to the whites.

All saw there would be war ; and Lord Dun-
more, the Gov-er-nor of Vir-gin-ia, raised a large force
from the land west of the moun-tains, and sent them
to quell the foe.   This force, which was but four
hun-dred strong, did but lit-tle good.

The gov-er-nor now saw that his on-ly chance
was to raise a force large e-nough to kill off most of
the tribe, and so make peace sure for the time to
come.   For this he raised some three thous-and

men, from all parts of Vir-gin-ia.   This ar-my was in two parts, one un-der the gov-er-nor, and the oth-er un-der Cap-tain Lew-is.

It was on a bright clear morn in the month of Oc-to-ber, that Gov-er-nor Dun-more float-ed his part of the force down the fair O-hi-o to the Hock-ing. This is, you know, the queen month of all the year in these parts ; and in those days, ere the axe or the plough had shorn it of its wild charms, no spot in all the earth could have been more love-ly than that through which those brave Vir-gin-ians sailed on their way, for all they knew, to death.

Gov-er-nor Dun-more had sent word to Cap-tain Da-vis to meet him near the In-dian towns on the Sci-o-to, where it was thought the two bands could burn the towns and quell the Red men for all time.

On the 9th of Oc-to-ber, just be-fore the sun set, two men of Cap-tain Lew-is' band were out in the woods a few miles from camp on the hunt, when they were shot at by a small band of Red men. One was killed, but the oth-er ran, and in time reached the camp.   On the next morn, the 10th, there was a great fight, which was kept up through the whole day.   In it much blood was shed, and the loss on both sides was great.   The In-dians were led by a brave chief, called Corn-stalk, and at times through the long day, his voice was heard to ring out clear and firm, so that it could be heard by our men a-bove the din of the fight. " Be strong ! Be

AN IN-DIAN WAR-RIOR.

strong !" This war cry seemed to put new life in-to his men.

On the next day, when the dead had been cared

for, Lew-is left Point Pleas-ant, the scene of this sad
fight, and marched to meet the gov-er-nor.

As soon as Gov-er-nor Dun-more reached the
place he had start-ed for, he set his men to work to
build a strong fort. This was so well made that it
formed a safe home for the troops as long as they
had to stay in the place. On its top waved the Eng-
lish flag; and it was named Fort Char-lotte, for the
queen who ruled in Eng-land at that time.

The fight at Point Pleas-ant had been a hard one
for the In-dians; and when they saw the strong fort,
and knew that the great ar-my with-in its walls would
in a few days burn their towns to the ground, they
were filled with fear, and sent men to the fort to beg
the white men to spare their homes. The gov-er-
nor was a good man, and knew that the Red men
had been bad-ly used by these whites who had no
fear or love of God in their hearts; so he let them
come to him, and heard all they had to say.

But the proud Lo-gan would not go to the camp,
though he was but four miles a-way, at the Shaw-nee
town on the banks of the Sci-o-to. He sent his
speech in a belt of wam-pum, to be read to Lord
Dun-more by a chief in his tribe. In the shade of a
great oak, on the farm of Mr. Wolf, this grand speech
was read to the gov-er-nor. The tree still stood,
a few years a-go, in a field sev-en miles south from

Cir-cle-ville. I hope it still lives, a fair green shrine to the brave In-dian chief from whom some white men would do well to learn.

As the chief gave the speech, one of Lord Dun-more's men wrote it down, bit by bit, so we still have it as it came from the lips of the chief.

LO-GAN.

Lo-gan's speech :—" I ap-peal to a-ny white man to say if he ev-er en-tered Lo-gan's cab-in hun-gry, and he gave him no meat ; if he ev-er came cold and na-ked, and he clothed him not. Dur-ing the course of the last long and blood-y war, Lo-gan re-mained i-dle in his cab-in, an ad-vo-cate of peace. Such was my love for the whites, that my coun-try-men point-ed as they passed, and said : 'Lo-gan is the friend of the white man.' I ev-en thought to have lived with you, but for the in-ju-ries of one man. Col-o-nel Cres-ap, the last spring, in cold blood and un-pro-voked, mur-dered all the re-la-tions of Lo-gan, not ev-en spar-ing my wo-men and chil-dren. This called on me for re-venge. I have sought it. I have killed ma-ny. I have ful-ly glut-ted my ven-geance. For my coun-try, I ful-ly re-joice at the beams of peace. But do not har-bor the thought that mine is the joy of fear. Lo-gan nev-er felt fear. He will not turn on his heel to save his life. Who is there to mourn for Lo-gan? Not one!"

This trea-ty at Fort Char-lotte was kept but a short time, for the war of the Re-vo-lu-tion now raged in our land, and the Eng-lish did all they could to get the In-dians to fight on their side.

One nice thing is told of Lo-gan, the brave and proud chief, which I am sure ev-er-y boy and girl will like, and which shows us that a kind heart beat un-der his dark skin.

At one time a Mr. Brown lived with his dear ones in a log hut not far from Lo-gan's home. Mrs. Brown had a lit-tle girl who was just learn-ing to walk, but the dear babe had no shoes to save the soft feet, and they were far from a place where such things could be bought. One day Lo-gan came to the hut as a guest to Mr. Brown; and as he with a smile watched the lit-tle child who knew and loved him, and so tried to show him how well she could walk, he begged Mrs. Brown to let her go up with him, and spend the day at his cab-in. The child of whom he seemed so fond threw her arms a-bout his

LO-GAN BRINGS THE CHILD BACK.

neck, and was read-y to start at once ; but poor Mrs. Brown was not so well pleased. She feared that she might not see her babe soon if she let her go ; still, she dared not show her fear, so she put on a smile which I fear was not a bright one, and at last let Lo-gan have his way.

That day was a long one to the sad wife, and as the hours passed she grew more and more ill at ease. But to her great joy just as the sun went to rest back of the red clouds, and the birds were say-ing their pray-ers ere they went to bed, she saw Lo-gan with the child in his arms a short way from her door. He brought her in ; and as he put her down to the floor, she ran to Mrs. Brown, and with glee showed a rich pair of moc-ca-sins on her lit-tle feet, which the chief had made for her with his own hands.

CHAPTER VI.

THE SIEGE AT FORT HENRY.

In the first days of the war the In-dians were not sure which side they should fight for ; so the Brit-ish sent Col-o-nel Guy John-son by the way of Can-a-da and De-troit to bribe the Ir-o-quois In-dians to help them. At this time, these In-dians were known as

IN-DI-ANS BURN A CAB-IN.

the Five Na-tions, as they were made up of five tribes. Each of these was fond of war, and all were glad of the fine things which the Eng-lish gave them.

They did not like the poor men of our land, for they had been taught to fear them; and now seemed a good time to pay them up for all their proud deeds. So they fought on for the Brit-ish, as a pack of hounds would go for the game of their mas-ter, with no hope of a real good to their tribes. In time the wise chiefs took this view of the case, and more than one told the Eng-lish of it.

One brave deed should find a place in this book ere we leave this sad In-dian part of the his-to-ry of our State.

The State of Vir-gin-ia had quite a large fort on the banks of the O-hi-o, but a few yards from where Wheel-ing now stands. It was called Fort Hen-ry, for Pat-rick Hen-ry, the bright Gov-er-nor of that State. The fence which held the fort was eight feet high, and made of great logs placed on end. In the yard which this formed was a good well, a store-house for food and pow-der, and homes for the sol-diers of the fort. Out-side this fence were thir-ty or more log cab-ins for the set-tlers who tilled the land near at hand, and raised large herds of cows and hors-es on the grass land which they had cleared.

SI-MON GIR-TY.

Now that the men were need-ed in the war, but for-ty were left in the fort. One half of these were old men, and the rest young boys. With the In-dians was a white man named Gir-ty. This man was dressed like the Red men, ev-en to the war-paint and plumes; and with his dark skin stained to match theirs it would be hard to tell him from the rest of the tribe. He was at first a brave scout with Gen-er-al Lew-is; but for some cause that proud, hard man hit him one day while in his head-quar-ters so that the blood ran down his cheeks. Gir-ty left the room; but just as he reached the door he turned, fixed his eyes up-on the gen-er-al, and said, " Your quar-ters, sir, shall swim in blood for this !" Then he went and joined the In-dians, and did all he could to hurt the whites.

Now Gir-ty knew the state of Fort Hen-ry, and made up his mind to take it. Five hun-dred In-dians led by him, would, he thought, make short work with a fort held by for-ty old men and young boys. So the Brit-ish gave them good guns, and sent them on their way.

Col-o-nel Da-vid Shep-herd, who was head of the fort, was a brave, firm man. Though there was not much pow-der in the fort, there was a large mass stored in a house but six-ty yards from its door.

On the morn of the 26th of Sep-tem-ber, 1777,

word spread through the town that In-dians had been seen in the woods not far off ; and in a short time all the folks in the place caught up such things as were near at hand, and made a rush for the fort. They slept there that night ; and the next morn Col-o-nel Shep-herd sent word to a near place for more men. Then he sent a white man and a ne-gro to a lot near by to bring in some hors-es. The white man was killed by shot from the In-dians' guns, but the ne-gro ran back, and reached the fort pale with fright, but not harmed.

When Col-o-nel Shep-herd heard of this, he sent out four-teen men to drive off the In-dians. They passed through a corn-field, and down to the banks of the riv-er, where they were out of reach of the fort, —when four or five hun-dred In-dians rushed on them, and e-lev-en were killed at once. Though Cap-tain Ma-son had a bad wound, he made out to creep in-to a heap of logs and brush, and laid there till the In-dians left the place. Two of his men did the same. Col-o-nel Shep-herd heard the guns, and sent Cap-tain O-gle with twelve more men to help the first, for he did not think the foe so great. O-gle was met by the In-dians so that he could not go back, and eight of his men were killed. The Cap-tain had a wound, and hid in a bush ; while three of his men ran for the woods and were saved. Thus you see that of the for-ty men who held the fort, but ten were left. The wom-en in those sad days could fire guns quite as well as the men ; so they were of use in the siege.

Now Gir-ty with his whole force rushed for the fort ; but the shots which reached him, though few, were so well aimed that they took down some of his best men, so that the In-dians did not like to go on. He saw that he must change his plan now, so he placed a few of his men in each house of the town, and told them to fire through the doors and win-dows to-wards the fort. They kept up a strong fire on the fort for some time, when Gir-ty came to the door of one of the cab-ins with a white flag in his hand, and called to the fort to give up in the name of the King of Eng-land. The white flag, or "flag of truce," you know, is used in war when one side has some-thing to say to the oth-er ; and while it is held no shots are fired. When Gir-ty saw that the fort did not mean to give in to his pow-er, he said he would kill ev-er-y one it held when he did take it. Col-o-nel Shep-herd then came to one of the port holes, and cried that they would not give it up as long as a man was left to keep it.

CHAPTER VII.

ELIZABETH ZANE.

THEN the shot flew like rain, and the In-dians fell as fast as they came with-in sight of the fort.

This was a love-ly day in fall,—clear, calm, and bright ; and here in the land God had made as fair as a-ny spot on earth, it seemed strange and out of place that such a fight and wild blood-shed should go on.

For six long hours it waged fierce and strong. At last Gir-ty saw he could not take the fort in that way, so looked a-bout him for some help. Then a bright plan came to his mind. At the black-smith's shop he found some large i-ron hoops ; and he hoped to make a can-non by means of these. So he took a great log of oak, dug out the in-side, and bound it in a firm way with the hoops. This he filled with slugs of i-ron, and placed it so that it would knock down the gate of the fort. He looked out to keep a long way from it when it was fired ; but some of the In-dians, who had no fear of it, stood near to see it work. When the match was touched to it, the great gun

IN-DIAN WAR DANCE.

flew in-to a hun-dred bits, and killed or wound-ed all
the In-dians near it! A loud yell told the folk in
the fort that all was not well with the foe.

At one time the pow-der was low in the fort, and
it was seen that some one must go for more to the
house where it was stored, which you know was six-
ty yards out-side the gate.

The task was so hard that Col-o-nel Shep-herd
did not like to tell one of his men to go, but asked
who would. A num-ber of the young men said they
would ; but there were so few in the fort he did not
feel that he could let more than one out-side the walls
at a time.

While they talked of it, a young girl, E-liz-a-beth
Zane by name, came to the front and said she would
go. Her broth-er Si-las tried hard to keep her back,
and told her that a man would be more fleet. She
said they had not a man to spare from the fort, and
that if she should fall she would not be missed.
Then she took off those clothes which would be in
her way as she ran, and passed out through the gate.
The In-dians when they saw her bound forth, did
not fire a gun, but called in a loud voice, "Squaw!
squaw! squaw!" In the house to which she was to
go, was one of her broth-ers with a few oth-er friends.
It had not been ta-ken by the In-dians, as it stood a
short way from the rest of the cab-ins, and was in a

line of the port holes of the fort. So they feared they should be shot if they went that way, and did not try it. When E-liz-a-beth told what she had come for, her broth-er took a ta-ble cloth, and tied it to her waist; then he poured in-to it a keg of pow-der. As she came out of the house the In-dians fired at her; but swift as a deer she sped on, and reached the fort as sound as she had left it. With this brave deed of the young girl came new hope to the hearts of the men, and they fought with more will for the rest of the day.

When night came on, the In-dians, tired out, rushed off to the woods to build their camp fires and fill the night air with their war whoops and wild songs. The poor folk in the fort sank to rest, used up by their hard day's work.

In some way word reached the A-mer-i-can lines not far off; and just at sun-rise on the next morn a band of for-ty men rode up to the gate of the fort. The brave Gen-er-al Da-vid McCul-loch, who led these, was in some way cut off from the main troop, and had a hard ride to save his life. The In-dians knew what a brave man he had been, and wished to take him a-live; so they did not shoot, but the whole band set chase and tried to cut him off, and thus make him theirs. His was a long, dar-ing ride, and at times his last chance seemed gone; but down the

ES-CAPE OF GEN-ER-AL M'CUL-LOCH.

rocks and through the brush, the well trained steed held his way, till at last, horse and man reached the foot of the steep hill, and rushed for the thick wood. Through this he at last made his way back to camp, where he had been mourned as dead.

The In-dians now saw that with the new men in the fort they could not take it; so they burned the cab-ins in the town, killed all the cows and horses they could find, and then left.

Such was the sad end of the storm of war which burst on the qui-et town on that bright Oc-to-ber day. The storm passed on, but it left the whole town in ru-ins, blood, death, tears; and with most of the small band in the fort, a life-long woe.

CHAPTER VIII.

MEN MEET TO TALK OF OHIO.

New Eng-land, as I have said, was well filled with whites; while the whole broad West was still left to the Red men. Great towns had sprung up all a-long the coast, and wise men were found in each place to start a col-lege or school, to preach of God, or make laws to help men hold their rights. The great war of the Rev-o-lu-tion was fought, and Eng-land had let go her hold on our land, so at least it was free.

But the great war which had earned us our freedom had made life hard for most men in our land.

Gold was scarce. The men who had been to the war and were used to camp life, did not like to go back to their farms, and work hard with hoe and spade. They had learned to drink and laze by the side of the great camp fires when not in fight, and hard work did not suit them now.

Wash-ing-ton was at the head of our land at this time, and it took all his wise thoughts to know just what to do with these bad men.

He had oth-er things to fill his mind which were quite as hard to fix. The men who were wise and brave, who did not fall in-to the sad straits of the first, need-ed, and were well worth, the thought he could give to them. The of-fi-cers who led the men to the fights, who planned how the foe was to fall, —these were the ones who would make ours the first land on the earth, and these were the ones Wash-ing-ton wished to place where they could do the most good. All through the long war these men had no pay in gold; on-ly notes which were said to be worth so much in gold. But when the war was done no gold was left in the land to pay these notes.

Wash-ing-ton and the men who made the laws at Con-gress looked to O-hi-o and those States just west of it as a help in this. They felt it but fair to these men who had done so much for our land to give them a part of the great west in place of the gold they would not get. Con-gress went so far as to tell how much land each should have; but as there were doubts in the minds of some as to the right of these men to give this land, no place was set a-part for that end.

In 1785, Gen-er-al Ben-ja-min Tup-per with some friends went to the land which now forms the south and east part of O-hi-o, to lay out points for towns. The East was full; and men were to be found in the south part of New Eng-land who wished to go West to live.

In Jan-u-a-ry, 1786, Gen-er-al Tup-per came home. One cold night while the snow blew in great drifts a-cross the fields, and the wind roared and shook at the win-dows, and sent great tongues of flame up the wide throat of the chim-ney, he sat in

ROOM IN PUT-NAM'S HOUSE.

front of the blaz-ing fire in Gen-er-al Put-nam's room, in deep talk with that brave man.

For some time Gen-er-al Ru-fus Put-nam had thought it well to push west in-to this land he had heard praised so much ; but not till Gen-er-al Tup-per's call on that cold night had the thing seemed so real.

So it was that these two brave men who had fought side by side to free our land from her foe, now talked far in-to the night of the fair place which they wished to fill with brave, good men, so that in long years to come it should be the pride of our great land. Would that those good men could now see the fruit of that night's talk!

When they had laid a few plans, they wrote a piece which came out in a Bos-ton pa-per on the 25th of that same month. This urged all good men who had a wish to go to new lands, all of-fi-cers and men who had served in the late war, to form an "O-hi-o Com-pa-ny," and buy the land they had so long thought would be theirs by right, and so help build up a new State. The piece spoke of the rich soil, and the fine crops it would be sure to yield ; of the mild, soft air,—and in fact gave to the spot all the praise it could. It was signed by Ru-fus Put-nam and Ben-ja-min Tup-per, and went on to ask all who wished to know more of the scheme to meet on Feb-ru-a-ry 15, and choose men to go to the grand meet-ing which would be held at the Bunch of Grapes inn, in Bos-ton, on March 1, 1786. The men who met here were Man-as-seh Cut-ler, Win-throp Sar-gent and John Mills, John Brooks and Thom-as Cush-

ing, Ben-ja-min Tup-per, Crock-er Samp-son, Ru-fus
Put-nam, Jel-a-li-el Wood-bridge and John Pat-ter-
son, and A-bra-ham Wil-liams.   They thought and
talked well, and at last formed a plan by which gold
could be raised to buy the land, and build homes for
the men who should go there to live.

In a year's time, on March 8, 1787, these men
met once more in Bos-ton.   At first they were to
have none but Mass-a-chu-setts men in the col-o-ny ;
but these could not raise all the gold need-ed, so now
it was thought best to take such men from Con-nec-
ti-cut, Rhode Is-land, and New Hamp-shire, as
cared to buy up shares of the stock ; for with-out the
gold these men saw they could not push on the
cause.

CHAPTER IX.

HOW THEY BOUGHT THE LAND.

With these new men the funds were raised to a
good sum, though not as large as was at first wished ;
and the com-pa-ny thought it best to send at once to
Con-gress to buy the land north and west of the
O-hi-o Riv-er.   They chose one of the best men in
New Eng-land to do this ; the Rev. Man-as-seh Cut-

ler, the pas-tor of a small church in what is now
Ham-il-ton, Mass-a-chu-setts.

Doc-tor Cut-ler was a bright, firm man, who knew
a great deal of men's ways, and could make him-self
liked by all who saw him. The
work he had to do with Con-gress
would need just these things.

At this time the slaves in the
North had all been freed; and the
South knew that New Eng-land
and the States near her thought it
a sin to keep the poor blacks so
low. But she had paid gold for
her slaves, just as she had for her
hors-es and cows, and did not like
to give them up. So it was that
the slave law was felt in those
days, and the South wished to
make all the new States which
came in, slave States, so that they
would be on her side, and help
her keep her slaves.

COR-NER SHELVES IN DOC-
TOR CUT-LER'S HOUSE.

Doc-tor Cut-ler and those who
sent him did not wish this new land to bear such
a taint; and he worked hard and well to get a law
passed by which no slaves could be kept in the
place. This was the best thing which could have

been done for our whole land; and O-hi-o, with the
whole North in fact, can-not give too great thanks
to the brave coun-try par-son for the great work he
did for them on that day.

Though this was the great thing he had to do,
there was still one more; which, no doubt, was
thought quite as much of by those who looked
to-wards the West for a home. This was to get as
much land, and on as good terms as he could, for the
new col-o-ny. He did both of these so well, that
men of to-day praise his work.

He bought a large lot of land on the O-hi-o Riv-
er for one dol-lar an a-cre, while for all bad lands he
was to pay less than half that price. Then he urged
Con-gress to give some land, which when leased
would help keep a col-lege. A lot of land one mile
square was thrown in for each town-ship to pay for a
school, and one of the same kind for a church.
What could have been added which would be worth
more than these grants? When a land starts with
the rule that schools and church-es shall be a part of
its life, it is sure to grow good and strong sons in its
midst.

Doc-tor Cut-ler was much pleased with what he
had done, for he had great faith in the scheme. He
thought the new land he and his friends were to
found, would one day be the fin-est in the world, and

told the men so. At this time he wrote a book in which he told for one thing what he thought O-hi-o would be in one hun-dred years from that time. He said that the "O-hi-o and Miss-is-sip-pi would be more load-ed than any streams on the earth," and went so far as to add that boats moved by steam would be used on these grand riv-ers. The steam-boat was not known in those days, and had not been heard of on this side of the sea .

Doc-tor Cut-ler did not put his name to the book; but it was read and talked a-bout by men in all parts of New Eng-land, and no doubt led some to this place who would not have cared to come had it not been for his words.

Some men there were who had no faith in it; and these laughed and sneered at "Put-nam's Par-a-dise," or "Cut-ler's In-dian Heav-en," as the wags of the day chose to call the whole O-hi-o plan. They did not think the soil as good as that in their own State, and said these men ought to have seen as much of the Red men as they cared to. The O-hi-o Com-pa-ny paid no heed to these, but once in so long a space of time met at the "Bunch of Grapes," and made plans for their new home. They thought the best point for the ci-ty which was sure to grow from their col-o-ny, would be where the Mus-king-um joined the O-hi-o; and there they made a plan,—on pa-per,—of the ci-ty of Mar-i-et-ta, which was to be.

CHAPTER X.

WHY IT WAS CALLED THE BUCK-EYE STATE.

The first band to go West was to start in the fall of 1787; but it was not till the first day of the last month of that year that they left Dan-vers, Mass. These went first to make boats, which would take the whole band up the stream; and Ma-jor Haf-field White led the way.

The next par-ty went from Hart-ford, Conn., on the 1st of Jan-u-a-ry, 1788. The days were short and cold, and the moun-tains were clothed with deep snow, so this band had a hard time to make its way. But on the 14th of Feb-ru-ary they came up with White's par-ty, and all worked on the boats for a month.

On the 1st of A-pril, the whole fleet, made up of three log boats, one flat, and one large ship which they called the *May-flow-er*, sailed down the stream. This voy-age seemed bright and full of joy to them. The days were warm and bright, and as they sailed

WHITE'S FLEET ON THE O-HI-O.

on, a few wild flow-ers were seen on the banks of the stream.   They must have been a glad band when on A-pril 7th, 1788, they made for the shore, and land-ed on the site of Mar-i-et-ta, and thus be-gun the large and grand old " Buck-eye State."

With this band was one fine, tall man who had been brave in the past war, and had such a grand walk, that the Red men who met them on the bank were at once quite struck by his mien, and so called him " He-tuck," or " big Buck-eye."   This man was Eb-en-e-zer Sproat; and it is not hard to see that the name which was first meant for him, might soon be made to stand for all the band of which he was a part.

One more tale is told of the way the State got its name.   The sto-ry goes that as the *May-flow-er* reached the shore, two young men sprang to the bank, and tried to see which should cut down the first tree,—for the land must be cleared, you know, to make space for the homes they were to start.   One of these, Jer-vis Cut-ler, a lad of 16, and son of the Rev. Ma-nas-seh Cut-ler, chose a buck-eye, which cuts with ease; while the oth-er in his haste took a tree of hard wood.   The buck-eye was the first to come to the ground; hence the State took its name from that.

CHAPTER XI.

THE FIRST HOME OF THESE MEN.

As soon as they had reached the land, Gen-er-al Put-nam, who was the head of the band, set the men at work to build a fort. This must be strong to keep the Red men at bay, and at the same time make a good home for all. The gen-er-al had much taste in such things; and this fort when it was done was said to be the best of its kind west of the moun-tains. It was a long house which ran on four sides of a square. In the midst was a space left o-pen to the sun and air. At the ends, and half way from these, were small square rooms, each of which formed a kind of tow-er; while in each small box-like top were four square holes through which the foe could be spied while still far off. The whole was built of boards which they had brought from the East, as tight and strong as it could be made. All a-round this was a high fence of logs, set on ends to keep the In-dians off. This was called "Cam-pus Mar-ti-us," and was the home of these men for five long years. It was cut up in-to sev-en-ty and two rooms, and would hold nine hun-dred men if need be.

CAM-PUS MAR-TI-US.

Now a name was to be found for the ci-ty they were to build, and all sorts were thought of by the men. France had helped in the war just passed, and all in our land felt the debt they owed her. So when some one said it might be well to name their ci-ty for the fair queen, Ma-rie An-toi-nette, who ruled France at that time, all were pleased with the thought; and Mar-i-et-ta thus had its name.

At the close of the first year, ma-ny brave and well learned men had come to Mar-i-et-ta to live. Of these, Ar-thur St. Clair, the Gov-er-nor of the ter-ri-to-ry, Re-turn Jon-a-than Meigs, who in the years to come was made Gov-er-nor of the State; Gen-er-al Ben-ja-min Tup-per, and Com-mo-dore A-bra-ham Whip-ple, of Rhode Is-land, who led the band which burned the Gas-pee in Nar-ra-gan-sett Bay in 1772, were the best known.

On the 15th of Ju-ly, Gov-er-nor St. Clair with some of the wise men read the laws which were to guide the folks in the new town. On the 25th, a law was made by which each man in the place was forced to spend a few days of each year in war drill, so that in time of need they would know how to meet the foe.

At first there were but for-ty and eight men in the place, but at the end of the year there were one hun-dred and thir-ty and two, as eigh-ty and four men had joined through the year.

While they were at work on this fort, the men lived in tents, or in huts made from the limbs of trees. One great tent was used by Gen-er-al Put-nam as a kind of town hall; and here most of the brain and law work of the place was done. W h e n the cold months came, food was scarce and hard to g e t. No flour was to be found in the place, and out of hulled c o r n or coarse meal was made all the bread used.

The bears a n d d e e r which h a d form=d meat food for

AN OLD WIND MILL.

the men were few and hard to find, as the In-dians lived on these as well as the whites; but our men bore these things as brave men do, and in the spring plant-ed more corn and grain, and looked for a full crop in the fall.

By the spring of 1791 three more towns had been formed near Mar-i-et-ta ; one at Bel-pré, a rich tract of land at the mouth of the Lit-tle Hock-hock-ing, one at Wa-ter-ford, and the last at Mil-lers-bor-ough, a few miles from Mar-i-et-ta. At the last place the first mill in O-hi-o was built, and in it was ground the meal for all these towns.

CHAPTER XII.

THE FIRST SCHOOL IN OHIO.

MUSKINGUM ACADEMY.

N 1797 a pa-per with Ru-fus Put-nam's name at its head was passed from man to man, that each might give as he felt he could for the fund which was to pay for a school-house in the place. Small schools had been held in Cam-pus Mar-ti-us, but now there was felt a need of a school for the large boys and girls. In 1800 the house was done; and the Mus-king-um A-cad-e-my, the first high school in O-hi-o, was o-pened. Da-vid Put-nam, a grad-u-ate of Yale, was its first teach-er.

Ships had been built by some of these men when they lived in New Eng-land, and now with fine

GEN-ER-AL RU-FUS PUT-NAM'S HOUSE.

wood on the banks of the streams, it seemed quite like home for them to make ships here in the heart of A-mer-i-ca. Some of them were used to the ways of men " who go down to the sea in ships," and some few had sailed on most of the seas on our globe ere they came to this port, two thous-and miles from the o-cean by way of the riv-ers. But you have read e-nough of these brave men to know that they did not give up for small things, and so the ships were one by one built on the edge of our fair streams and float-ed down to the sea.   One old cap-tain used to tell with much fun of an Eng-lish of-fi-cer who would not be-lieve that he came from A-mer-i-ca, as he was quite sure there was no such port as Mar-i-et-ta on our coast.   The cap-tain tried in vain to tell him where the place was, but at last was forced to take the map, and point out the place, then with his fin-ger trace his course down the stream till at last he reached the mouth of the Miss-is-sip-pi.   The awe of the of-fi-cer was so great that the cap-tain al-ways laughed when he thought of it.

A short time af-ter the O-hi-o Com-pa-ny had bought this land, Judge Symmes of New Jer-sey bought a large tract of land on the O-hi-o Riv-er near the mouth of the Great Mi-am-i ; and at the same time Ma-jor Stites of Penn-syl-va-nia made a home for his men at the spot where the Lit-tle Mi-am-i flows in-to the O-hi-o.

He brought his twen-ty or thir-ty men here in the fall of 1788, and made a block house for them to live in.   This was next to the first town made in O-hi-o. A-mong these were Col-o-nel Spen-cer, Ma-jor Ga-no, Judge Go-forth, Fran-cis Dun-la-vy, Ma-jor Kib-bey, Rev. John Smith, Judge Fos-ter, Col-o-nel Brown,

Mr. Hub-bell, Cap-tain Flinn, Ja-cob White, and John Ri-ley. These were all strong, brave men, and at the time it seemed that the town they formed would be the great ci-ty of the West; but this was not to be, as you will learn as you read on.

CHAPTER XIII.

HOW THE CHAIN OF FORTS WAS BUILT.

MEN first came to live on the spot where Cin-cin-na-ti now stands, on De-cem-ber 28, 1788. They were led by Ma-thi-as Den-man, of Spring-field, New Jer-sey; and all of them came from that State.

In 1790 Ma-jor Dough-ty built a fort here which he called Fort Wash-ing-ton; and in the same year Gov-er-nor St. Clair laid out Ham-il-ton Coun-ty, and made the seat of it at Cin-cin-na-ti, which at that time was called Lo-san-ti-ville. He changed the name to the one it now has in hon-or of the so-ci-e-ty of the " Cin-cin-na-ti," which was made up of some of the best men who had fought in the last war. That so-ci-e-ty still lives, and men think it a great hon-or to have their names on its roll.

The men in these parts tried hard to live at peace with the Red men, and at last coaxed the In-dians

SPY ON THE LOOK-OUT.

to say they would be friends and do what was right, if the white men would do the same. This was put on pa-per and signed by the men of the towns. Then the In-dian chiefs placed their marks at its end. These marks meant the same as their names, and in fact took the place of them, as none of the Red men knew how to write. But in a short time it was seen that they cared naught for the word they gave. All through the warm months of 1790 they went to the towns when they could get the chance, killed the folks, and stole what they could find. At times whole boat-loads of men were killed by these foes.

Gov-er-nor St. Clair found out in some way that they were to fall up-on our men as soon as the chance came, so to stop this he sent a large force to meet them ; but no real good came from this, and in the cold months of 1790 and 1791 each town had all it could do to keep off these bad Red men. All who had small homes and farms in the State were forced to leave them, and live with their friends in the block hous-es at Mar-i-et-ta, Bel-pre, and Wa-ter-ford. Brave men were sent out as spies, and these gave word when the foe was near.

As all the land north of the O-hi-o, and far up on the shores of the great lakes, was filled with these Red men, fear was felt at one time that they might join in so strong a band as to kill all the whites in the towns on the O-hi-o and its branch-es. So at last Gov-er-nor St. Clair was told by Con-gress to take two thous-and men, and make a chain of forts from the source of the Mau-mee to Fort Wash-ing-ton. He did as he was told to, and made his first stop at Fort Ham-il-ton. Then he moved on to a spot for-ty-two miles from there, where he built Fort Jef-fer-son. Once more he moved on, but with on-ly a part of his men ; and ere he had time to build his fort or get word to the rest of his force, the foe came up-on him, and a hard bat-tle was fought, in which he lost eight hun-dred men. Those who were spared hid in the woods and by stealth made their way back to Fort Jef-fer-son.

Some thought Gen-er-al St. Clair was to blame for this great loss of men, and so he lost most of his friends ; but the best and wise men of the land said that he did as well as an-y one in his place could have done. This bat-tle was fought on No-vem-ber 4, 1791.

Gen-er-al An-tho-ny Wayne was made to take his place, and in De-cem-ber 1793, he went with a strong force to build the fort St. Clair had failed to do. They reached the spot on De-cem-ber 25, and a sad Christ-mas day it was to them. The ground was free from snow, and as they came out of the woods near the spot where the bat-tle had been fought, they

GEN-ER-AL ST. CLAIR.

found the whole place strewn with the bones of the dead. Six hun-dred skulls were picked up, and these with the oth-er bones were placed in the earth ere the first work on the fort was done. When it was built Gen-er-al Wayne called it Fort Re-cov-er-y.

RU-INS OF FORT RE-COV-ER-Y IN 1810.

In the warm months of 1794, he built Fort De-fi-ance, on the spot where the Au-glaize and the Mau-mee join.

On Au-gust 20 of that year, he won in a hard fight known as the " Bat-tle of Fal-len Tim-bers ;" but it was not till Au-gust 3, 1795, that this long war with the Red men came to a close. Now a trea-ty was made at Green-ville, in which most of the In-dians joined. It gave peace to the white men, and told the Red men just what part of the land they should have as their own.

CHAPTER XIV.

CINCINNATI.

HE sec-ond band of men who came to the Mi-am-i were led by Ma-thi-as Den-man and Rob-ert Pat-ter-son; and were but twelve or fif-teen in all. They had a hard time on the riv-er, as it was cold, and the ice in the form of great cakes float-ed down the stream, and at times knocked their boat out of her course; but at last they reached the north bank of the O-hi-o just across from the mouth of the Lick-ing. They came here to form a trad-ing post, and had made plans of this, and the town they were to start, ere they left their home at Lime-stone.

The name which they gave to the place was, as you know, " Lo-san-ti-ville," which was made up by a strange man from a-cross the sea. We do not know his name, and I think you will say you do not care to know it. The name of the town was formed, as he said, from the words *Le os ante ville,* which meant, so he said, "the vil-lage op-po-site the mouth." We are glad Gov-er-nor St. Clair had the good sense to change this for the fine one it now has.

As soon as these men came to the spot they were to call home, they made three or four cab-ins; the first of which was built on Front, east of and near Main Street. Both the high and low land was full of trees, and through these dense woods the streets were laid out. The points where they joined were marked by trees, and in them deer were of-ten seen, and shot by both the In-dians and the white men. It seems strange, does it not, that less than a hun-dred years a-go, wild an-i-mals should roam at will on

A DEER HUNT.

the spot where now the fin-est ci-ty of the West rears
its proud head? Yet such was the fact.

The town then stretched from East-ern row—
now Broad-way—to West-ern row; and from the
riv-er as far north as North-ern row, now Sev-enth

HOW THEIR GRAND-PAR-ENTS WENT TO CHURCH.

Street. More than half of the men in the place
joined St. Clair's band, and most of them were
killed; so for a time the place did not seem to grow.

But fif-ty men came to live here in 1792, and a
church was then built. This was the Pres-by-te-ri-an

Church, which stood till the year 1847, when it was ta-ken down, and its tim-bers used in the hous-es of that part of Cin-cin-na-ti called Tex-as. When first built it was a firm house, but not large in size. No plas-ter was to be seen on its walls, and its floors were of boat planks laid on great blocks of wood.

While war was in the land, the men took their guns to church and held them at their sides just as their grand-fath-ers had done in years gone by, in the small log meet-ing house in far off Con-nec-ti-cut. This church was in time fixed up in a good style. The Rev. James Kem-per was the first to preach in it, and was its pas-tor for some years.

When Gen-er-al Wayne came, he made the camp for his troops in a place half way from Cin-cin-na-ti to Mill Creek. To this he gave the name of " Hob-son's Choice," as it was the one spot he found good for a camp. Here he and his troops stayed for months ; then he moved them to a spot in Darke coun-ty, where he built Fort Green-ville, the place where the great trea-ty was made.

The block house which was made by the first men who came to Cin-cin-na-ti was called Fort Wash-ing-ton, and stretched from Third to Fourth streets, and east of Broad-way, which was then a mere lane. It was formed of great hewn logs which were built in-to cab-ins, a sto-ry and a half high.

These were the homes of the men. Some of the cab-ins were large, and had nice things in them, and were used by the of-fi-cers of the fort.

On the north side of Fourth Street, just a-cross from the fort, was a large plain house with a fine gar-den at its back. It was the home of Col-o-nel Sar-gent. On the east side of the fort, Doc-tor Al-

li-son had a plain frame house in the midst of a fine, large g a r - d e n. This was known as Peach Grove. Not far from Col--o- n e l Sar-gent's home on Fourth Street, a n d just a-cross from where St. Paul's Church

THE SCHOOL-HOUSE.

now stands, was once the small frame school-house where the young of the town were taught. The jail was on the north side of the square.

On the 9th of No-vem-ber, 1793, the first pa-per print-ed in O-hi-o was start-ed at Cin-cin-na-ti, by Wil-liam Max-well, and was called "The Sen-ti-nel of the North West-ern Ter-ri-to-ry." It was a small pa-per, and in three years changed its name to

" Free-man's Jour-nal." On the 11th of Jan-u-a-ry, 1794, the first line of boats made the trip from this place to Pitts-burgh. The two boats were small, and each made a trip once in four weeks. They were cov-ered to keep off the shot which at times the In-dians still fired at craft on the stream, and had small port holes in the sides for guns which were used at such times. In 1801, the first ship built for the sea at Mar-i-et-ta, passed down the O-hi-o filled with grain. A crowd stood on the banks of the stream at Cin-cin-na-ti to watch it as it sailed past.

When the streams were ice bound in the cold months, the men and boys made their way from place to place on skates, and oft-times called at the In-dian towns on these to buy game or meat. At such times the ska-ter if he was good at his art, would show off his skill to the Red men who stood on the bank, and watched with joy his strange feats.

In Jan-u-a-ry, 1802, Cin-cin-na-ti was made a town ; and in 1819 it was made a ci-ty. In 1795 it had but nine-ty and four cab-ins, ten frame hous-es, and some five hun-dred folks lived in the place; but it did not stop here. In the next fif-teen years it had grown so much that there were five times that num-ber of men in its homes.

The first child born in the place was Wil-liam Moo-dy. Ba-by Moo-dy first saw the light of day

THE SKA-TER.

on March 17, 1790; and the change which took place in the town of his birth from the time he could just trot through the woods, then all a-round his house, to that of his death in 1879, seemed more like some fai-ry tale than a bit of real life in our plain world.

CHAPTER XV.

HOME LIFE OF THE FIRST MEN IN OHIO.

As you have learned, the homes of these men were small, rude log cab-ins, which at first were joined in the form of a block house or fort; but in time the need of the fort was not felt, and then the cab-ins were placed on the spot of land a man wished to make in-to a farm for him-self.

The men who lived in the new land were friends, and glad to help each oth-er, when they could. When a man was to build a house, he would tell his friends, and they would all join and help him. In this way the work did not take long, and all liked the fun which the "house-raising," as they called it, was sure to give. The first thing which was done at such times, was to make the chim-ney. This was of stone, with a great wide fire-place left at its base; and was placed at one end of the house. Here was

LOG CAB-IN.

to be made the fire which should warm the whole house in the cold, i-cy time of the O-hi-o win-ter; and here were to be cooked the great roasts of bear's meat, or the sweet steaks of the deer; while the rab-bit stew, or the wild tur-key stuffed with its rich force-meat, would at times send forth its sweet smell in-to the small room.

There was much wood on the land in those days, and grand fires were built in those wide mouthed chim-neys. The men had no nails, and so made pegs of wood to take their place. Boards for chairs, shelves,

FIRE-PLACE AND OV-EN.

and ta-bles, as well as for floors, were hewn out of logs with the axe. The hin-ges and latch for the door were made of wood. To this latch was tied a string which passed through a hole in the door and hung on the out-side. When this was pulled the door latch was raised, and the door could be pushed o-pen; but at night the latch string was drawn through, and so the door was locked.

The beds were bunks like those in a ship, built to the side of the house; and all the chairs, stools,

and ta-bles were made at home in the cold months, or on days when the rain kept the men in doors. In those times the buck-eye was a great prize to the men. Hats were made from shreds of its bark, trays were carved from its trunk, and spoons and bowls for the young folks' sup-per of bread and milk were made from

BA-BY.

its wood. Great troughs were hewn from the large trunks, which served to catch the sap of the ma-ple trees in the spring, and were used as cra-dles for the babes through the rest of the year.

All the cloth used in the State was made at home. Girls were taught to spin and weave when they were quite young, and a new dress was much more prized then than it is now. When girls had to make the cloth as well as the dress at home, and with their own hands at that, they found that five yards would take the place of the twen-ty yards used to-day. In the warm

AN OLD MILL.

months flax was used for this, but in cold times wool took its place. The men's clothes were made at home as well, and the cloth was spun and wo-ven like that for their wives.

No stoves were used, and match-es were not known. Fire brands were kept through the night, and used to light the fire on the next morn. When these gave out, a " flint and steel" was used in its place.   Guns were kept hung up-on pins of wood ; and the wife could use these when a wild tur-key or deer or bear made a call at her door.   The In-dians were still to be seen near the place at times, and the wives liked to feel that they had a gun at hand in case it was called for.

Corn bread took the place of the fine wheat bread now in use ; and all who have tast-ed of the sweet " pone " baked in front of the fire on a smooth board, will say that no bread of to-day is half as good.   The folks of those days lived bright lives, were full of health and good spir-its, and made the best of their hard lot.

CHAPTER XVI.

THE TOWN WHICH THE FRENCH MADE.

In May or June of 1790, Jo-el Bar-low went to the lands a-cross the sea to try and get men to come to the O-hi-o and make homes.   He was sent by the " Sci-o-to Com-pa-ny," who had formed a plan to buy land not far from Mar-i-et-ta, and then sell it to these men at a high price. Bar-low first went to Par-is, and there praised the lands he wished to sell. The French are a bright, gay race, who like new things; and they were much pleased with the tale he told of the far West. That all Par-is should learn of his plan, he had bills print-ed in the French tongue, and sent to all parts of the ci-ty. These bills gave such a bright tale of the place it seems strange that none were to be found who did not think them quite true. All thought that Bar-low's West must be the one fair spot in all the world. The bills said that O-hi-o had a fine fresh air; and so warm were the cold months that frost was not known. A riv-er called the "Beau-ti-ful," and filled with fish of vast size, flowed through the land. Here trees grew which gave all the su-gar they might need; and a kind of shrub was found there up-on which can-dles grew. This was the Wax Myr-tle, or, as it is called in New Eng-land and some parts of our land, the "Bay-ber-ry" bush. Deer filled the woods; and here the hunt for them was not made hard by the fox, li-on, or ti-ger. Swine would roam through the woods, and feed on the grass and wild grain, and thus cost the men no care or gold.

There were no tax-es to pay in this fine land, and men here were not forced to learn the arts of war, as they were in France.

This was a fine view that Bar-low's bill gave them; and the French were so pleased that some sold all they had, and bought of Bar-low land in O-hi-o.

In his bill he for-got to state that the trees must be cut down ere the land would yield its large crops; and that if there were no li-ons, in their place were In-dians far worse than these wild beasts. So the French-men, who had lived in Par-is all their lives, took their wives and chil-dren and came to our land.

These were not fit to live the hard life men were forced to live in this place. They had been used to in-door work. Some of them had put the gold on the paint in the king's rooms, some had made fine chairs, or a coach for the rich men to ride in, and a few were well learned in the books of the time; but no more than a small part of the band knew the least thing of farm work. As some were found who would like to come, but had no gold to pay for the land, and the Sci-o-to Com-pa-ny wished a large band to come to their lands, they said that to all such they would give fif-ty a-cres of land, a house, and a cow. For this the men were to work for the com-pa-ny three years.

To urge men to buy the land, Bar-low had a map made, and stained with bright paints, which he said gave a good view of the place. A cop-y of this map is owned by Mr. J. P. R. Bu-reau, of Gal-li-po-lis, who was one of the first to come here.

BAR-LOW'S MAP.

As soon as the Sci-o-to Com-pa-ny found that a large band of French-men, some five hundred in all, were on their way to the Sci-o-to lands, they hired the O-hi-o Com-pa-ny to clear the trees and build a few hous-es for the new men.

When the O-hi-o Com-pa-ny had been here but a short time, they laid out a small town, called "First Town" on the map, but by them named Fair Ha-ven. As the ground here was low, and the place might be wet in the spring, they placed the town they were now to build four miles down the stream from this, and up-on a high bank. They worked hard to clear a great square, and on it they built eigh-ty log cab-ins one sto-ry high, which they placed twen-ty in a row, with a street or space be-tween them. At each cor-ner they made a strong block house twice as high.

It is said that Col-o-nel Rob-ert Saf-ford cut down the first tree. The small curved breast-work near the bank of the stream was thrown up for the men to flee to in case the foe came to them while they were at work on the town. At the right

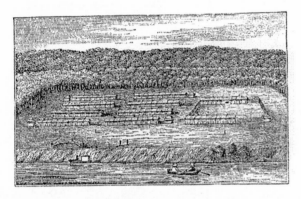

GAL-LI-PO-LIS IN 1791.

of these small cab-ins were two rows of large ones, for the rich men who were to make their homes here. At each end of these rows was a block house, and these were joined by a strong fence made of great logs placed on end and close to each oth-er. One of these cab-ins was made for a ball room, and one for a town hall.

Ru-fus Put-nam, who saw to all this, was hired by the Sci-o-to Com-pa-ny to do it; but they failed to pay him for his work, and so he lost a large sum, as he had to pay his own gold to the men who helped him.

In 1791, these French-men first saw the land which they were to call home. They had a hard time on their way to the place, and so were tired when they first caught sight of the new log cab-ins they were to live in. It is safe to say that they were not as well pleased with this view of the real town, which they called Gal-li-po-lis, as they had been with the one they had drawn in their mind, from the bright tales told by Bar-low some months be-fore in far off France. They had hard times from the first; for they had not thought they must pay gold for all they ate the first year, while they cleared the ground for the seed they had brought a-cross the sea; but they were brave, and tried to be light of heart. They helped each of their friends in all the ways they could, and so made the best of the lot which had been forced up-on them. The In-dians tried them some, but they were not such foes to the French as to the men at Mar-i-et-ta.

In time the hard things they were forced to bear made them sad and home-sick. When the cold months came, they found the land they had paid for in France was not theirs at all. The gold which Bar-low took he had kept, and with it had run off to

Eng-land; so now the Sci-o-to Com-pa-ny failed, and the poor men had no gold to go back to France, and no land here to call their own.

The cold was so great that win-ter, that the O-hi-o was a bed of ice. The deer and bears went to the woods far South, and the men who hunt-ed for them had no meat to sell to the white men. The flour had all been used in the fall, and now there was naught to live up-on. One man, his wife, and sev-en chil-dren, lived for a week or more on dried beans, boiled with no salt or grease, and no bread. These were folks who had been used to nice things in France, quite as you are to-day. Some died from hun-ger, and some from cold. At last a man was sent to Con-gress to tell of their wrongs; and that bod-y felt for the lone folk, so far from their own land and friends, and so gave them a large tract of land to use for their farms.

CHAPTER XVII.

"ZANE'S TRACE."

In May, 1796, Con-gress passed a law by which Eb-e-ne-zer Zane was to make a road from Wheel-ing in Vir-gin-ia, to a place in Ken-tuck-y. The next year, Mr. Zane, with his broth-er, and son-in-law, John M'In-tire, made the road ; which was not wide nor smooth, but could be used by horse-men, and no more was wished for.

Now for this act Zane was to have three farms, each one mile square. These were to be where men could cross the riv-ers; and he must keep boats at these points for such as wished to use them, if he would keep his farms. One was to be on the Mus-king-um, one at Hock-hock-ing, and the third on the Sci-o-to.

For the first Mr. Zane thought the best place would be at Dun-can's falls; but he saw what a fine spot for a town was the site on which Zanes-ville now stands, so he had his cross-ing here, and made his farm take in the falls. Then he took for his next the land which lies just a-cross from Chil-li-coth-e. This he thought was not as rich land as the oth-ers, so he gave it to his broth-er, as pay for his part of the work on the road. For the third he chose the spot on which Lan-cas-ter has since been built.

The boat which Mr. Zane used to take his men a-cross the stream was a strange one,—two ca-noes placed side by side, lashed a-cross with a stick. The fer-ry o-ver the Mus-king-um was where the up-per bridge is now built, and the ford for horse-men to cross was near the site of the dam.

FIRST INN AT ZANES-VILLE.

As Mr. Zane could not see to all his work, he had Wil-liam M'Cul-loch and Hen-ry Crooks move to this spot and tend the fer-ry. The first mail in O-hi-o was brought from Mar-i-et-ta to M'Cul-loch's cab-in by Dan-iel Con-vers in 1798.

When Mr. Zane laid out the town he called it West-bourn ; but when the mails were brought to M'Cul-loch's cab-in, Con-gress made that a post-of-fice, and called it Zanes-ville.

At this time, when men from far off came to these small towns in the West, they were glad to get a fur rug or a blank-et, and a spot on the floor near the fire, for a bed. This did not seem to M'Cul-loch and his good wife quite the right way to make men like the land. He thought much of this, and at last made his house an inn for the time. This was a real home for the tired men who came here, and was the first inn in the place. Here one was sure of a bed with fresh sheets, and a clean sweet room to sleep in. It was not strange that men rode a long way from their course to stop at M'Cul-loch's cab-in for a night's rest.

The small log cab-in once had for a guest Lou-is Phil-lipe, who was in time made King of France ; and this was an hon-or of which most of the large inns in the land would have been proud.

In 1802, Dan-iel Har-vey built a large inn in

Zanes-ville where Third and Main streets now join ; and when it was done M'Cul-loch closed his house to all but his friends, and made it a qui-et home once more.   Har-vey's house was the first with a shin-gled roof, built in the town.

In the year 1788, some men chose the spot where Day-ton now stands for a town, which they were to

call Ven-ice. They wished to buy this land, a n d m a k e homes on it at once. But the In-dian war which soon raged in the land made these men think it not wise to bring their wives and chil-dren to such a place, and as no

VIEW IN DAY-TON, 1840.

one else cared to come, Ven-ice was not formed.

In 1795, when Wayne's trea-ty had been made, and the war was a thing of the past, Gen-er-als Jon-a-than Day-ton, Ar-thur St. Clair, James Wil-kin-son, and Col-o-nel Is-ra-el Lud-low, bought all the land on the Mi-a-mis, near the mouth of the Mad Riv-er ; and on the 4th of No-vem-ber laid out the town of Day-ton.   The lots were marked out, and a small price set for them.

On A-pril 1, 1796, nine-teen men came to live in the place. In 1803, there were but five men who had their homes here, yet it was made the seat of Mont-gom-e-ry coun-ty. The oth-er men had made their homes on farms near by, but could not be said to live in the town. With this, Day-ton soon grew to be a large town; and far back in 1808 it had a news-pa-per. Though this was but a small sheet, in size like those boys print for fun, no doubt the folks of Day-ton were well pleased, and, in fact, proud of this joint work of Messrs. M'Clure and Smith, as the prin-ters were named.

CHAPTER XVIII.

MORE TOWNS FORMED AT THIS TIME.

In Ju-ly, 1787, Con-gress gave three large tracts of land to the Mo-ra-vi-an men who spent their lives in teach-ing the In-dians to love God, and do His will. These tracts were to be used as homes for such In-dians.

In those far off times, there were men in the South who felt it was wrong to keep slaves; and of these were most of the men who went to two

FIRED AT BY IN-DIANS.

church-es in Ken-tuck-y. They were led by the
Rev. Rob-ert W. Fin-ley, who freed all his slaves,
and urged his friends to do the same, and then go
with him to O-hi-o, where, as you know, none could
be kept. He wished to go to a fine part of that
land ; so he wrote to Col-o-nel Mas-sey, who owned
much land in O-hi-o, to ask him where he had best

VIEW OF CHIL-LI-COTH-E, 1840.

go. Mr. Mas-sey was so much pleased with this
that he set a day to meet these men, and then went
with them to see the land ; but the In-dians met the
band, and some white men were killed. The rest
did not like to live near to such foes, and so no town
was made for the time.

But in 1796 the Rev. Mr. Fin-ley formed a band

of men to make a home here; and some of these were to go in the spring of the year, and raise a crop of corn at the mouth of Paint Creek. These left their homes by the first of A-pril. Some went through the woods, while the rest made their way up the streams in boats; and in Au-gust, 1796, Chil-li-coth-e was laid out.

In this town which was laid out and set-tled by men who loved God, and strove to do His will, the first re-lig-ious news-pa-per in A-mer-i-ca had its birth. It was called " The Re-cord-er," and the first num-ber came out in 1814.

The first men who came to this land chose fair spots for their homes. They loved the great trees and shin-ing streams which flowed on through soft green banks fringed with wild flow-ers. They had few things to make their hard lives bright, and so took all the joy they could from the fair things near them. Though it does seem that they were led by some pow-er not seen, to choose the rare spots in our State for the sites of those towns which in time were to be the great cit-ies of our wide land, they left much just as God made it, for men of our day to find and use. In fact there are few spots in this fair-est of States which are not gems in their way, and worth all the praise one can give them. You, my young friends, will see as you grow old, and look a-round this great world that there are few pla-ces in it as bright or as fair as your own dear State.

Man-ches-ter was laid out in 1791, by Na-than-iel Mas-sey. In De-cem-ber, 1794, Is-ra-el Lud-low, laid out on part of the land bought by J. C. Symmes, the first plat of the town

HAM-IL-TON IN 1840.

of Ham-il-ton, which at first he called Fair-field. In a short time a few men came to live here, but it was some years ere the place grew to an-y size.

SHA-KERS DANC-ING.

H e n-r y Tay-lor built a mill on Tur-tle Creek in the spring of 1796, half way from Cin-cin-na-ti to Day-ton, where he ground all the corn raised on the farms near both these towns. This was close to the spot where Leb-a-non now stands. In 1803, that town was laid out, and a strange town it was ; for on-ly one house, and that a log cab-in, was to be found in the place.

But in those days men looked at a spot, marked off its streets, squares, and house-lots, and then shut their eyes, and thought how it would look ten or more years to come, when each lot had a house on it, and the streets were filled with men and young folks.

Just four miles west of Leb-a-non is Un-ion Village, which was formed by the "Sha-kers" in 1805, and is still the home of that strange folk, who have such odd views of life and God.

CHAPTER XIX.

A HOME IN THE NORTH.

At this time, that is in the year 1796, James Kings-bu-ry—who, though born in Con-nec-ti-cut, had spent most of his life in New Hamp-shire,— grew tired of the hard, rock-y farm on which he had toiled, and set out with his wife and three chil-dren, the old-est not four years of age, to try his luck in the far West.

He had heard much of the rich land near the lakes, and wished to see how it would seem to farm on such soil. He put his goods, food, and tools, in a stout farm wag-on, which was drawn by a yoke of ox-en. A cow was hitched to the back of this to give them milk on their way. His wife and chil-dren rode on his one horse, while he and a young broth-er whom he took with him to help on the way, drove the ox-en by turns.

They were forced to go at a slow rate of speed, and at night to sleep on the ground. A great fire was made when they camped for the night, to keep off the wolves which at that time were to be found in our woods. By this, too, the wife cooked their meal; while the lit-tle folks, glad to use their small, cramped legs, ran and played at her side. But one in the camp was forced to keep up, and tend the fi r e each night, and they no doubt took turns at this.

CAMP ON THE LAKE-SIDE.

In time they came to a few log huts on the spot where now stands the large ci-ty of Os-we-go. Here Mr. Kings-bu-ry had a large flat boat built; and when it was done put his wife, chil-dren, and goods on board, and then made his

way up the lake.　The boy stayed on shore, and
drove the cow and ox-en through the woods.　At
night they would all meet at some point on the
shore, and camp on the beach.　When they reached
Fort Ni-ag-a-ra, which was as far as they wished to
go on Lake On-ta-ri-o, they took the boat which had
served them so well, placed it on the wag-on, and so
dragged it some thir-ty miles to Lake E-rie.　At the
spot where Buf-fa-lo now stands they met Gen-er-al
Mo-ses Cleve-land, for whom the ci-ty of Cleve-land
was named.

Gen-er-al Cleve-land was the a-gent for a band of
men who had just bought a vast tract of land in the
north part of what is now O-hi-o ; and he urged
Kings-bu-ry to live on this tract.　So it came to pass
that James Kings-bu-ry was the first white man who
made his home in that part of the State.

He chose what he thought was a fine site for his
home, and hoped, as did Gen-er-al Cleve-land, that
in time he would see a great town spring up near
him.　When his log cab-in was built, Cleve-land and
his men went on to choose a site for one more great
town which all felt would soon be built in this north
land.

They sailed down the edge of the lake till the
Gen-er-al saw the fine broad stretch of land which
told him he had reached his goal.　Then he went

back to Con-ne-aut, where Kings-bu-ry had made his
home, and in the course of two short months the ci-ty
of Cleve-land was laid out in the form of a map.
This same map was found a few years a-go by Ex-
Gov-er-nor Hol-ley of Con-nec-ti-cut, who was the son
of one of Cleve-land's band. Its date was Oc-to-ber
1st, 1796, and the streets which were marked on it
bore the same names as those of to-day.

Kings-bu-ry had a sad time in his home in Con-
ne-aut. Food was scarce; and just as the cold of
the first win-ter came on, he was forced to go back
to his old home in New Hamp-shire for a short
space of time. He would be back by the first of
De-cem-ber, he said; so with a kiss for his wife and
lit-tle ones, and a word of trust to the lad, he rode
out of sight.

The cold winds blew, and snow came soon that
year. As weeks grew to months, and no one came
to the small cab-in in that lone spot, both Mrs.
Kings-bu-ry and her broth-er feared that harm had
come to their dear one. But they could not quite
give up all hope, and watched each day in hopes
that he would come back.

At this time a great storm set in, and for days
the great bank of snow a-round the house crept up
to-wards the top till naught but the roof and part of
one side could be seen, if there had been an-y one to

THE CAB-IN IN WIN-TER.

look at it. But there was not; the In-dians who sold meat to the Kings-bu-rys had gone South, where the cold was not so great, and the food in the small cab-in grew less and less as the weeks went on. A new babe came to them at this time, and,—weak, cold, and ill,—the poor wife found it hard to keep her hope.

At last on Christ-mas Eve, that bles-sed night of all the year, as she went to the door and looked off in-to the woods and longed for their dear one, she thought she saw some-thing move. You may be sure her heart beat fast as she watched the far-off speck. Yes, it was Mr. Kings-bu-ry! he was walk-ing to-wards the house, for his horse had died from cold some way back. He had a bag of flour on his back which he had bought at the last town, for he had feared all was not well at his home. He had been ill all this time, and had not known how time had passed.

The cold still held its sway; and as the long win-ter dragged on, the cow died. The new babe, who had lived on its milk, now had naught to eat; so it pined a-way and at last starved to death. It was a sad day for that small band when the poor lit-tle thing was placed in a small box, and laid to rest in a grave not far from the house.

When the warm months brought Gen-er-al

Cleve-land's band back to lay out the spot for their new town, Mr. Kings-bu-ry moved to that place that he might have friends near at hand in case of need. He built his cab-in on a spot not far from the site of the Post Of-fice.   On the ground near at hand, where the Ci-ty Hall and the Ca-the-dral now stand, he raised his first crop of corn.

The next man to make a home here was Lo-ren-zo Car-ter.   These two homes, which held but nine souls, were all there was of Cleve-land in 1797. How ma-ny are there to-day? and yet that was not a hun-dred years a-go.

CHAPTER XX.

THE FIRST MAZEPPA.

SOME five miles north and east of Bell-fon-taine, at the head of the Mad Riv-er, is a lone grave; which a few years a-go was closed in by a fence of wood.   On the small slab which marks it are the words:

"In mem-o-ry of Gen-er-al Si-mon Ken-ton, who was born A-pril 3, 1755, in Cul-pep-per coun-ty, Vir-gin-ia, and died A-pril 29, 1836, aged 81 years and 26 days.   His fel-low cit-i-zens of the West will

long re-mem-ber him as the skil-ful pi-o-neer of
ear-ly times, the brave sol-dier, and the hon-est
man."

Si-mon Ken-ton was but a youth when he came
out to Ken-tuck-y in the year 1771. He was in
fights with the In-dians from that time till the trea-ty
at Green-ville, and ma-ny of the brave deeds which
he did are like fai-ry tales of the Blue Beard style.
As he was the first and real Ma-zep-pa, the sto-ry of
his wild ride should be known by ev-e-ry O-hi-o boy
and girl.

At one time, when he had been in these parts
some years and had had ma-ny fights with the In-
dians, he set out to do a rash thing, and came near
los-ing his life for it. Joined with Al-ex-an-der
Mont-gom-e-ry and George Clark, he made his way
to-wards the land of the Red men; and for what,
do you think? To steal hors-es from the In-dians.
These three went straight to Chil-li-coth-e, where
they knew was a drove of fine hors-es; and at night
caught and dashed off with sev-en,—a "pret-ty good
haul," we should say.

With all the speed they could, they made for the
O-hi-o; but when they reached the riv-er the wind
blew a gale, and the waves ran so high the hors-es
could not be forced to take to the wa-ter. It was
then late at night, so they rode back in-to the hills

and turned their hors-es loose to graze. On the next day they went once more to the riv-er, but their hors-es had had such a fright the night be-fore, that, though the wa-ter was now qui-et, they could not be forced to swim a-cross.

What should they do? They knew that the In-dians must have missed their hors-es long be-fore this, and were e-ven now on their trail. In a short time they thought it best to try to keep but the one horse each man rode and let the oth-ers go; so they made off for the ford above the falls, and no doubt they would have reached home in safe-ty had not greed for the oth-er four hors-es made them turn back once more. No In-dians were in sight, and they thought it a shame to leave these now when they had brought them thus far.

But some time had passed since they had let them loose, and it was no light work to catch them a-gain. The three men went in-to the woods, each tak-ing his own way. Si-mon Ken-ton was caught, and Mont-gom-er-y was killed while try-ing to save his friend,—while on-ly George Clarke made his way home. It is true Si-mon Ken-ton fought well for his life, but there were ma-ny In-dians, and he was soon seized and bound.

A sad night was that spent on the banks of the O-hi-o with his wild foes, but sad-der yet were to

come to the young man. He must have wished
more than once that he had left the hors-es a-lone,
as the long hours of dark-ness sped on. When the
day came, Ken-ton saw that the In-dians were in
high glee, as if some great thing was to be seen.
Could it be they were to kill him then and there?
Poor fel-low! he was sad of heart as he thought
what might be in store for him; but at last he felt
sure this at least was not his fate.

From what he could make out, they were a-bout
to go back to Chil-li-coth-e. When they were to set
off they caught the wild-est horse in the lot and set
Ken-ton on his back. The horse would not stand,
so it took a num-ber of the In-dians to hold him,
while oth-ers lashed Ken-ton on his back. They
first took a rope and tied his legs to-geth-er un-der
the horse, then they tied his arms. One rope they
put a-round his neck,—ty-ing an end to the horse's
head and one to his tail. They had much fun while
fix-ing the man and horse for the frol-ic, and would
yell and scream a-bout him, ask-ing him " if he would
like to steal any more hors-es."

Last, a pair of moc-ca-sins were drawn o-ver his
hands, so that he could not ward off the brush and
bri-ers he must meet on his ride.

When all was rea-dy, the horse and ri-der were
turned loose in the woods. Poor Ken-ton! it was a

hard ride he took that day. The horse kicked and jumped, reared and plunged, all to no use. At last, tired out, he fol-lowed the In-dians on their way back to Chil-li-coth-e. When Ken-ton was ta-ken from the horse's back, he was forced to run be-tween two long lines of In-dians who had clubs in their hands and used them in no light way on his back and head.

Then at last, when he had borne all this, he was told he must die. His clothes had been torn from him, and na-ked and bleed-ing he lay up-on the ground that night and gave up all hopes of life. When the In-dians met the next day to fix the place where he should be burned, they were not all of one mind. Some wished to make him a kind of state sac-ri-fice, so that those of oth-er tribes might en-joy the sight; and for this they thought it best to take him to Wap-a-to-mi-ka, a town some miles off. They passed through Pic-a-way and Ma-co-chee on their way, and ma-ny In-dians from these towns joined them to see the white man burned.

All hope had now fled, and Ken-ton felt sure of his doom, when a friend in the form of Si-mon Gir-ty came to his aid. Gir-ty had known him years be-fore; and though a bad man, had still a warm spot in his heart for his old friend. So he urged the chiefs to save Ken-ton's life, and they at last let him have his way.

Ken-ton had oth-er hair-breadth es-capes, but at last died in qui-et, in a small log cab-in near the spot where he now rests. His is but one link in the long chain of wild tales which the ear-ly his-to-ry of our State would make, if one had but the time to trace them out and join them.

CHAPTER XXI.

OHIO MADE A STATE.

ALL through these first days of war and strife, O-hi-o, though called by that name, was not a State, but a part of the North-west Ter-ri-to-ry. Con-nec-ti-cut, as you know, claimed a part of the land; and no fixed lines had been drawn to show just how large O-hi-o should be.

In 1800, Con-nec-ti-cut gave up her claim to the land; and the next year, when the third Leg-is-la-ture of the North-west Ter-ri-to-ry met at Cin-cin-na-ti, a man named Worth-ing-ton was sent to Con-gress to urge that bod-y to make O-hi-o a State.

In 1802 the con-sti-tu-tion was made; and some

say that on the 29th of No-vem-ber, when that
consti-tu-tion was framed at Chil-li-coth-e, O-hi-o
was made a State; but the act which Con-gress
passed to make it such,
was signed by Pres-i-
dent Jef-fer-son on Feb-
ru-a-ry 19, 1803. It was by this act that O-hi-o was
made one of the U-nit-ed States. The great seal of
the State bears the date 1802.

At this time there was a man called Aa-ron
Burr, who wished much to be Pres-i-dent of the
U-nit-ed States in place of Thom-as Jef-fer-son.
He was at last made Vice-Pres-i-dent, and held
some oth-er high of-fi-ces in the land. But Burr
was a vain, bad man; and at last, through his bad
acts, he lost the faith of most men and so could hold
no place of trust. Then he made up his mind to go
to Mex-i-co, stir up a strife in that land, and form a
new gov-ern-ment of which he would make him-self
the head. He had hopes that Lou-is-i-an-a, which
at that time took up a large tract of land far west of
the Miss-is-sip-pi, would join in his scheme.

On a fair is-land in the O-hi-o, not far from Mar-
i-et-ta, lived a rich gen-tle-man, Her-man Blen-er-
has-sett by name. His home was like a pal-ace,
and was graced by his wife, a most gift-ed and
love-ly la-dy. To it came the fine folk for miles

a-round, and its fame was known all through the land.

It was to this home that Burr came; and by his smiles and fine talk, which none knew bet-ter how to use, he urged his host to lend him large sums of gold, and to join in his scheme. It is not thought that Blen-ner-has-sett knew that Burr meant to rob our land, or in fact do any bad thing. He was led to think they were to free Mex-i-co from her hard fate, and so was glad to help the cause. Some O-hi-o men joined Burr, but they soon left him when they heard that ten boat-loads of things which were to be used in the work, had been ta-ken on the Musk-ing-um; and that four more were seized at Mar-i-et-ta, by the U-nit-ed States troops.

In 1806 Blen-ner-has-sett was made a pris-on-er, and the troops sacked his fine house. They found his wine vaults, and drank till they were quite drunk; then they tore up or burnt all they could lay their hands on. One man fired a bul-let through the wall of a large hall, and the ball passed through the room where Mrs. Blen-ner-has-sett and her chil-dren were hid. The place was ru-ined and Mr. Blen-ner-has-sett with his fam-i-ly were forced to live in a new land. He died a poor man on a small is-land south of Eng-land.

Aa-ron Burr, of course, failed in his scheme, as

he had done in those be-fore it ; and at last died on
Stat-en Is-land a sad lone death, with none near
to care for him in his last hours. He was a bright
man, who made a host of friends; and he might
have done much for our land had he been a good
man as well.

CHAPTER XXII.

OHIO IN THE WAR OF 1812.

AL-THOUGH the Rev-o-lu-tion was a thing of the
past, and our land called her-self free, Eng-land did
not like to give up the soil she knew was worth so
much. Then too she felt sore that our men had
gained the good will of the rest of the known world;
so she did all in her pow-er to make this land ill at
ease.

The fact that the A-mer-i-cans spoke the same
tongue as the Eng-lish made life for those who went
to sea on ships hard for them. The king told his
cap-tains to board each A-mer-i-can ship they saw,
to see if she hid Eng-lish sail-ors who had run
a-way. He said he had a right to do this. Oft-
times when they were short of hands these Eng-lish
cap-tains were glad to steal our men to make up

their crew. They swore that the men were Eng-lish
and our ships could not hold them back. This was
called "Im-press-ing A-mer-i-can sea-men"; and
made our land ver-y an-gry with Eng-land.

This was but one of the ways in which the old
coun-try bore down up-on us, and at last A-mer-i-ca
said she would stand it no more. So a new war
was fought; which did not last long, I am glad to
say.

You know Can-a-da was still owned by Eng-
land, and from that land she thought it best to fight
ours. The States at the north were the ones in the
most dan-ger.

Late in the sum-mer of 1812, Gen-er-al Will-
iam Hull went from Day-ton with twelve hun-dred
O-hi-o men, called " Vol-un-teers," as they were not
a part of the small ar-my which our land keeps in
time of peace. They were glad to give their time,
and lives if need be, to save their coun-try. These,
with three hun-dred of the real ar-my, went up in-to
Can-a-da, but did not meet the foe, and at last went
back to De-troit, which was at that time a part of
O-hi-o.

When the foe came to this place, Gen-er-al
Hull's men, who had been read-y to fight for a long
time, begged him to fire up-on the Eng-lish; but he
would not, and sent out a white flag (a ta-ble cloth),

which you know was a flag of truce. He not on-ly gave up the town of De-troit, but the whole of the Mi-chi-gan ter-ri-to-ry. This was on Au-gust 16, 1812. He was tried at court, and the judge said he must be shot for this cow-ard-ly act; but the Pres-i-dent let him live, as he did some brave things in the Rev-o-lu-tion.

W. H. Harrison

Gen-er-al H a r - r i - son, who, the next year, was made com-man-der of the ar-my of the West, marched his men to Frank-lin-ton, O-hi-o, and made his home there for the cold months.

Though the win-ter was a cold and hard one, the men had an ea-sy time while they l i v e d   i n   c a m p. "Scouts" were sent out from time to time, but no Red men were to be found.   These scouts were men who roamed through the woods near the camp, to see if they could find signs of the Red men near at hand.   But the In-

SCOUTS.

dians kept a long way off; in fact most of them were in the South, where game was still to be found.

It was in the year 1812 that the State cap-i-tal was moved to Chil-li-coth-e, where it was to stay till it was moved to Co-lum-bus, in 1816. The first cap-i-tal had been here at Chil-li-coth-e from the year 1800 to 1810. Then Zanes-ville held that hon-or for the next two years.

CHAPTER XXIII.

THE END OF THE WAR IN OHIO.

Gen-er-al Proc-tor now made his way to Fort Ste-ven-son at Low-er San-dus-ky—now Fre-mont—and tried to take it.

Twelve miles from Fort Ste-ven-son was a stock-ade called Fort Sen-e-ca, in which were some hundred and for-ty men. Gen-er-al Har-ri-son held this as a place in which the new troops on their way to the seat of war should meet. From this point he could send men up or down the riv-er, to guard the folk of the San-dus-ky Val-ley.

When Gen-er-al Har-ri-son heard of Proc-tor's move, he sent word to Ma-jor Cro-gan, a brave young man, but twen-ty and one years of age, who had charge of the fort, to leave and take his men to Fort Sen-e-ca; but the word came too late. There were on-ly one hun-dred and fif-ty men with him

FORT SEN-E-CA.

and they had but one can-non; but they had great faith in their young lead-er, and tried to do as he bade them.

At the first move, Proc-tor called him to give up the fort, and thus save a great blood-shed; but the

THE GUN AT WORK.

brave Cro-gan called back that he would not give it up while one man was left,—and then there would be no more blood to shed. To keep the fact that he had but one can-non in the fort from the foe, Cro-gan had it fired first from one place, then from an-oth-er; and saw to it that it was at all times put to good use.

At last the Brit-ish thought to take the fort by storm. When the brave Ma-jor saw what the foe were to do, he had his can-non placed so that it should sweep the ditch through which the foe was to pass. When this ditch was full of men, he fired it to such good ef-fect that the Brit-ish were forced to leave, af-ter a loss of one hun-dred and fif-ty men;—while in the fort but one man was killed, and sev-en wound-ed.

Cro-gan was made a colo-nel for this brave deed, and the la-dies of Chil-li-coth-e gave him a fine sword.

Ol-i-ver Haz-ard Per-ry, of Rhode Is-land, had built at this time two war ships—the "Law-rence" and the "Ni-ag-a-ra"—and sev-en small craft, at E-rie, Penn-syl-va-nia. When these were done he made his way with them to Put-in-Bay.

Just as the sun rose on the tenth of Sep-tem-ber, the Brit-ish fleet was seen un-der full sail far off to the west. Com-mo-dore Per-ry formed his ships in line of bat-tle, set sail, and bore down up-on the foe. He raised his flag, with its mot-to " Don't give up the ship!" and cheer up-on cheer went up from the men as they saw it wave in the breeze. The wind was so light that e-lev-en o'clock came ere the two fleets were near e-nough to o-pen fire.

At last a bu-gle note was heard to sound from one of the foe's ships, and loud cheers burst from all their crews; then from the ships' sides came shot which rained down thick and fast up-on Com-mo-dore Per-ry's flag-ship, the " Law-rence." The wind was so light and from such a point, that none of the oth-er ships could come to her aid; and for two hours she lay un-der this dread-ful fire, till all the crew, save three or four, had been killed or wound-ed.

At two o'clock the " Ni-ag-a-ra" was brought up, and Per-ry made up his mind to shift his flag to that ship. So tak-ing it un-der his arm, he went in a small row-boat to the " Ni-ag-a-ra," un-der full fire from the Brit-ish guns.

The fight last-ed for three long hours; and when it came to an end all the foe's ships fell in-to the hands of the A-mer-i-cans. This was the first case known in which all the ships of the foe were giv-en up; but Com-mo-dore Per-ry in his qui-et way on-ly sent this mod-est word to Gen-er-al Har-ri-son, who was at Fort Meigs, "We have met the en-e-my, and they are ours."

A short time af-ter this Har-ri-son crossed to Can-a-da, and gained the bat-tle of the Thames. In it Te-cum-seh, the great In-dian chief, was killed; and Proc-tor fled.

From time to time the In-dians had made trea-ties by which they gave up parts of their land to the white men. At first they seemed to have no thought that in time all would in this way slip from their grasp; but as time went on they saw the towns of the white men dot their whole hunt-ing grounds, and then they looked for some way to stop the e-vil. It was in truth a sad fate to which the Red man was at last forced to look, and it meant death to himself and his loved ones, if the tide of white men could not be checked. The In-dian does not till the soil as white men do, but roams o-ver great tracts of land to get his food. Some raise small crops of corn it is true, but they live for the most part on game, large and small, and the fish they catch from day to day.

At the time that the war of 1812 be-gan, the chiefs and wise men of the tribes saw, as they looked out o-ver their land, that they must soon find some way to oust the white men, or their na-tion would be wiped out from the earth; so it is not strange that they were glad to take part with the Brit-ish, in the vain hope that if they gained their cause they would get back their lands. But to-ward the end of the strife the poor In-dians found that the Eng-lish cared naught for them, and were in fact less kind than the A-mer-i-cans. When the war came to its end, sad in-deed was their lot.

HE LOOKS OUT O-VER THE LAND.

Though they were a low, cru-el race, we can but feel some pit-y for these poor Red men who knew naught of God, or of the world to come. They did what they had been taught was right; and when they saw the end of their race was near, if the white men gained their grounds, it is not strange that they fought with all their might, and used all the ways they could think of to drive their foes from the land.

In 1814 the sec-ond In-dian trea-ty was made at Green-ville, and three years from this, in 1817, a large tract of land in the north and west part of O-hi-o was bought of the In-dians at less than four cents an a-cre. The next year saw the last trea-ty made with them at St. Ma-ry's.

The Wy-an-dots lived on the soil of the O-hi-o long be-fore the French or Eng-lish came, and though for long years they were a great tribe, in 1842 they were but eight hun-dred souls. They still lived on a grant of land at Up-per San-dus-ky, which for a-ges they had called home. But now they were forced to leave these homes and the graves of their fath-ers of which they thought so much, and go to their new home south west of Mis-sou-ri. So it was that the last In-dian ti-tle to O-hi-o land was ced-ed to the State in 1842.

Though there seems to be a vague i-de-a that ma-ny In-dians still live in O-hi-o, the fact is there are but few in our State. Mass-a-chu-setts has more than we; and those of Maine would num-ber twice as ma-ny as could be found in our whole State. But O-hi-o can-not be blamed if she is glad that there are so few with-in her lines. She had her full

share of In-dian war and blood-shed, and these Red
men were the cause of most of her woes.

CHAPTER XXIV.

THE OHIO CANAL.

WHEN the war of 1812 and the In-dian fights
were past, things in O-hi-o be-gan to grow bright.
Men who had heard of the rich soil, but dared not
come here from fear of the In-dians, now made their
homes in the towns, or took up farms in the wild
parts of the State. Some of the bright-est men in
the coun-try were of these; and O-hi-o was soon felt
to be a great pow-er in our land.

In 1817, New York be-gan to make the E-rie
Ca-nal; and this led O-hi-o to think it might be well
to join Lake E-rie with the O-hi-o riv-er. On Ju-ly
4, 1825, the O-hi-o Ca-nal was o-pened; which was
the first step that made Co-lum-bus the great ci-ty it
now is. In two years from this time it was o-pened
as far as Ak-ron. In those days men went from
place to place on ca-nal boats, as they now do by
cars; but the chief use of this great wa-ter-way was
to bring the crops and things made in the cen-tre of

the State, far from the riv-ers, to the coast or the great lakes.

It is said that one of the first things brought on the ca-nal to the town of Cleve-land was a boat-load of coal. The folks of the place had nev-er seen this

ON THE CA-NAL.

kind of fu-el, and did not care to try it. Why should they, when great trees grew at their doors, and wood was cheap and easy to get? The coal was not as clean or nice to use ; and, though a man went through the streets all day cry-ing "Coal, coal, here's your fine coal," he found none to buy.

At last, just as night came on, a man who kept an inn said he would take two or three bas-kets to try. For these he paid at the rate of two dol-lars a ton. This was the first step in the great coal trade of Cleve-land.

It was in 1822 that George Gra-ham, then a young man, came from his home in Penn-syl-va-nia and set-tled in Cin-cin-na-ti. He took prompt hold of the steam-boat trade, then just on its start, and did much to-wards mak-ing Cin-cin-na-ti the great com-mer-cial ci-ty it now is. He held ma-ny of-fi-ces of trust and es-teem, and his name, with that of Dan-iel Ga-no, who gave much to the new town, will ev-er be loved by the folk of the place.

In 1850 the rail-road from Xe-nia to Co-lum-bus was first used; and the next year the Cleve-land, Co-lum-bus, and Cin-cin-na-ti was made. In 1852 the cen-tral road to Zanes-ville was o-pened, and in a few months Co-lum-bus was joined to Pe-qua by rails. These were the first of that great net-work of roads which now reach-es all points in the State.

CHAPTER XXV.

COLUMBUS.

THIS fair ci-ty is one of the three towns in the U-nit-ed States born a cap-i-tal.

In 1812 Lyne Star-ling, James Johns-ton, Al-ex-an-der Mc-Laugh-lin, and John Kerr asked the men who had charge of the State to make a spot on the high bank of the Sci-o-to riv-er,—just east of Frank-lin-ton,—the place where the laws of the State should al-ways be made. At this time the place which they chose was filled with great trees, but they wished so much to have their cap-i-tol here that they gave to the State a large lot ten a-cres square, up-on which the State build-ings were to be placed. Then they gave large sums of gold to be used in build-ing these; so it was they had their way, and our fair cap-i-tal came to be here on the banks of the love-ly Sci-o-to.

It was on the 18th of June, the same day on which war was de-clared with Eng-land, that the first sale of lots in the new town was held. Then soon men came to live in the place. Deer and small game were still to be found in the woods near by,

HUN-TER AT NIGHT.

and men had to give but a day or two to the hunt,
to get all the meat they need-ed in their homes.

The first church was held in a cab-in on Spring
Street, which was built in 1814 on a lot of Dr.
Hoge's. This was used but a short time, as most
of the folk went to the church in Frank-lin-ton till
1818, when the first Pres-by-te-ri-an church was
formed, and a frame meet-ing-house was built on
Front Street, where Dr. Hoge preached. The
first Pres-by-te-ri-an church was built in 1825.

Dr. James Hoge, who was fath-er of the O-hi-o
Pres-by-te-ry, preached in this ci-ty for more than
fif-ty years; and did much good by his ear-nest work
and no-ble life.

The First Meth-o-dist Church was built in 1814,
on the same lot where the church of to-day stands.
It was a small house made of hewn logs, and was
used for a church on the Lord's Day, and a school
for the rest of the week. In 1819 the first court
house was built.

The first news-pa-per in Co-lum-bus was start-ed
in 1814. A bright band of men had come to live
here, and they were sure to keep up with the rest of
the world, though their town was new and had but
few homes in its midst.

Lyne Star-ling, one of the four men who first
came to this spot and chose it for their town, did all

in his pow-er to make it the fine ci-ty he wished it to be. While he lived, he gave to it his chief thought and much of his gold; and when he died in 1848 he left a large sum of gold for the build-ing of a Med-i-cal Col-lege, which is called by his name. Here Dr. Sam-u-el M. Smith was a pro-fes-sor for thir-ty years; and dur-ing the war he was Sur-geon Gen-er-al of O-hi-o. For the last twen-ty years of his life, he was Pres-i-dent of the Cen-tral O-hi-o Lu-na-tic As-y-lum.

When the first meet-ing was held in the mod-est brick State house in 1816, Co-lum-bus held but sev-en hun-dred souls. Rude log cab-ins and quaint, low roofed hous-es were built side by side; and great trees grew in the streets and all a-bout the homes. But the spot which Mr. Star-ling and his friends chose for our cap-i-tal was a fine one, and men flocked here from all parts of the land. Still it was not till 1826 that the town be-gan to grow as fast as its first set-tlers wished.

The cor-ner-stone of the fine cap-i-tol which stands in this ci-ty was laid by Gov-er-nor Mor-row on the Fourth of Ju-ly, 1836; but the house was not done till 1855. In that same year the old cap-i-tol was burned.

One of the not-ed pi-o-neers of Co-lum-bus was Da-vid W. Desh-ler, who by his gold and wise

A QUAINT, LOW-ROOFED HOUSE.

coun-sel did much for the young ci-ty. Mr. Desh-ler, though born at Al-len-town, Penn-syl-va-nia, in 1792, came to Co-lum-bus in 1817. He took for his wife Bet-sey Green, of Eas-ton, Penn-syl-va-nia, cous-in of John C. Green, of New Jer-sey, a la-dy whose fine mind and pure, no-ble life did quite as much as her hus-band's gold and sound ad-vice, for the town she had made her home.

To them was born in 1827 a son, Will-iam G. Desh-ler, the pres-ent pres-i-dent of the Na-tion-al Ex-change Bank of Co-lum-bus ; whose no-ble deeds of char-i-ty have made his name known all o-ver our land.

The "Co-lum-bus Fe-male Be-nev-o-lent So-ci-et-y" has had two great sums of gold from his hands, one in the name of his moth-er, and the oth-er in that of a dear lost daugh-ter, " Kate Desh-ler Hun-ter," which helps it spread its kind-ly aid to ma-ny who, with-out his gifts, would have been left to suf-fer and perhaps die. Would that the world had more men like Mr. Desh-ler! It is such names as his which help to bright-en the pag-es of our his-to-ry.

Some years a-go Dr. Lin-coln Good-ale gave to Co-lum-bus a fine large park, which adds much to the beau-ty of the ci-ty.

CHAPTER XXVI.

A NOTED PIONEER AND HIS SONS.

IT is too of-ten the case that the his-to-ry of a place deals on-ly with the strife and wars which have torn it from time to time, and so we learn a-lone of such men as have been brave with sword or gun. Though these should by no means be left out, there are oth-ers who may not have wield-ed the sword, yet have done quite as much for our land, and have as much or e-ven more claim on our love and re-spect.

Of these, those brave men and wo-men who gave up home and friends in the East, and came here to plan and lay out towns in this wild spot, that those who came af-ter them might en-joy the fruits of their work—theirs are the names we should keep bright in our his-to-ry and our thoughts.

Near the year 1800, Ben-ja-min M. Pi-att, then a young man, came with his bride, a young Vir-gin-ian of high birth, to live in Cin-cin-na-ti. Mr. Pi-att was a law-yer; and his sound sense and clear head soon made him take the lead in pub-lic af-fairs. In time he was made Judge; and with his law part-ner,

Nich-o-las Long-worth, Esq., did much for the ci-ty in its young days. It is said that Mrs. Pi-att had the first pi-an-o brought to Cin-cin-na-ti. She did not dream that her taste, and wish to have her chil-dren well taught in all the things she had learned in Vir-gin-ia, would be the first step to-wards mak-ing Cin-cin-na-ti the mu-sic cen-tre of the land ;—yet such was the case.

In the year 1828, Judge Pi-att bought a large farm on the small stream which the In-dians called Mac-o-chee, and on the spot where the In-dian vil-lage of that name once stood.

Mrs. Pi-att, whose taste was not con-fined to mu-sic a-lone, had the grounds laid out with great care ; a large tract be-ing filled with ro-ses and oth-er fine flow-ers. The place is still owned by Judge Pi-att's sons.

The eighth of these, the well-known schol-ar and writ-er, Donn

ON THE MAC-O-CHEE   Pi-att, was born in Cin-cin-na-ti, Jan-u-a-ry 29, 1819; he was taught at the Ath-e-næ-um,

now St. Xa-vi-er Col-lege, and la-ter stud-ied law.
While Pres-i-dent Pierce ruled our land, Mr. Pi-att
went to Par-is as sec-re-ta-ry to Mr. Ma-son, who
was Min-is-ter to France. As Mr. Ma-son soon be-
came too ill to at-tend to his du-ties, the whole
charge of af-fairs fell to Mr. Pi-att, and for more
than a year were left in his hands. Dur-ing this
time, his wife,—a bright la-dy, fair in face and mind,
—wrote un-der the name of
"Belle Smith" let-ters to the
New E-ra, of Wash-ing-ton,
then hav-ing for its head the
well-known Gam-a-li-el Bai-ly.
In time Donn Pi-att start-ed
a pa-per in Wash-ing-ton called
the *Cap-i-tal*, of which he was
the head for a long time.

The fine stur-dy traits of
the Judge are seen in this son,
who has ev-er been not-ed for
his firm, free views in the pol-

DONN PI-ATT.

i-tics of the coun-try and those things which go to
make up our ev-er-y day life.

At pres-ent Mr. Pi-att is the Ed-i-tor of *Belford's Mag-a-zine*, one of the lead-ing pow-ers in our
land. Like his fath-er, he is fond of the peace and
qui-et which farm life gives; and when tired and

worn by hard brain work, he flees to his home on
the Mac-o-chee; where, a-mong his friends, his
books, and his farm work, he gains the rest and
health which on-ly Dame Na-ture can give.

Two years young-er than Donn, is his broth-er,
A. San-ders Pi-att, one of the brave sons of O-hi-o.
He was taught at the same col-lege as his broth-er,
and, like him, had the best traits of both pa-rents.
When his school life was done, he chose to live on
the farm; and went back to his lands in the rich
val-ley of the Mac-o-chee, where he wrote or tilled
the soil, as he liked.

When the war of the Re-bel-lion broke out in
our land, he was one of the first to o-bey his coun-
try's call.   On A-pril 30, 1861, he was made Col-o-
nel of the Thir-teenth O-hi-o In-fan-try.   La-ter he
raised a reg-i-ment, and clothed and fed them for a
month and six days with his own gold.   This was
called the First Zou-ave Reg-i-ment, from the fact
that the men wore a fine red-leg-ged u-ni-form, which
they were soon forced to give up.

As Gen-er-al Pi-att did not join the ar-my with
the thought of mak-ing it his life work, af-ter much
brave fight-ing he left the field and went back to the
Mac-o-chee, where a large fam-i-ly of moth-er-less
chil-dren need-ed his care.   Here he can still be
found at work in his fields or in his pleas-ant stud-y.

J. Wy-koff Pi-att, the first son of Ben-ja-min, was one of the not-ed men of Cin-cin-na-ti, and ma-ny years a-go did a good deed for that ci-ty. As in most towns, when "fire" was cried, men and boys from all points rushed to the scene of the fire; and oft-times, by their wild yells and free use of wa-ter and the axe, did more harm than good. Mr. Pi-att saw this, and tried long to have the men who were to put out fires ev-er read-y at a call, and paid well for their work.

But the old style had a kind of Fourth-of-Ju-ly fun and frol-ic in it which most of the young folks did not like to give up. Though Mr. Pi-att lost ma-ny friends by his course, he at last gained his way; and now his worst foes, if they still live, would not go back to the old style if they could.

Mr. John J. Pi-att, a cous-in of this fam-i-ly, though not born in the State, is claimed by O-hi-o peo-ple. His po-ems have made his name known all through our land; while that of his wife, Sa-rah M. B. Pi-att, is al-so known and loved by all who read our Mag-a-zines.

CHAPTER XXVII.

OLD-TIME AMUSEMENTS IN OHIO.

THE chil-dren who lived in Cin-cin-na-ti fif-ty or six-ty years a-go had some a-muse-ments quite dif-fer-ent to those of the pres-ent day an-y-where.

There was a mu-se-um kept by a French-man named Dor-feuille—Door Fool! Was not that a fun-ny name?

He showed a num-ber of wax fig-ures like those in the E-den Mu-see—on-ly not so good, as im-prove-ments have been made in ev-er-y-thing late-ly, ev-en in wax fig-ures. Most of Mr. Door Fool's wax fig-ures were made by a young man named Hi-ram Pow-ers. He had a great nat-ur-al tal-ent for art, but was on-ly a ve-ry poor, ig-no-rant boy.

One day a rich man of Cin-cin-na-ti named Nich-o-las Long-worth saw the fig-ures in Door Fool's Mu-se-um, and asked who made them. He was told, and this kind and good Mr. Long-worth, see-ing that the poor boy had such tal-ent, sent him to It-a-ly to study the art of sculp-ture. Mr. Long-worth paid all the boy's ex-pen-ses, and was well

paid back when Pow-ers be-came a great sculp-tor—
the first A-mer-i-ca ev-er had to win fame.

His most fam-ous stat-ue was called "The Greek
Slave," and chil-dren may see cop-ies of it to this
day in art gal-ler-ies.

When they do, they should re-mem-ber that it
was made by Hi-ram Pow-ers, a poor boy who be-
gan life at a sal-a-ry of three dol-lars a week.

Fif-ty or six-ty years a-go it was thought that
Cin-cin-na-ti was go-ing to be the great-est ci-ty of
the West—that was why it was called "The Queen
Ci-ty of the West." It was the point to which
ev-er-y-bod-y and ev-er-y-thing was drawn.

The run-a-way slave es-cap-ing from Ken-tuck-y
be-came free if he could but get safe-ly a-cross the
broad O-hi-o Riv-er in-to Cin-cin-na-ti.

The cir-cus and thea-tre peo-ple made that ci-ty
their head-quar-ters. Bands of Ne-gro Min-strels
al-ways played there, and in one of them was a
young man as poor as Hi-ram Pow-ers,—on-ly Ed-win
For-rest got six dol-lars a week, ex-act-ly dou-ble the
pay of the young wax fig-ure mak-er. Ed-win For-
rest af-ter-wards be-came as great an act-or as Pow-ers
was an art-ist; but at the time of which we are writ-
ing, Ed-win For-rest was on-ly a trav-el-ling Ne-gro
Min-strel, and blacked his face and sang a song, at
the end of which he used to turn what cir-cus peo-ple

call a "Flip-flap"—some lit-tle boys would call it a som-er-sault. Boys should re-mem-ber how hum-ble was the be-gin-ning of these two great men, Ed-win For-rest and Hi-ram Pow-ers, and learn that per-se-ver-ance is as ne-ces-sa-ry to suc-cess in life as tal-ent.

There were ma-ny oth-er fam-ous peo-ple who are now called "The pi-o-neer the-at-ri-cals of the West."

Ma-ny of the chil-dren of these peo-ple have be-come known as well as their pa-rents. The Bate-man Sis-ters made a great rep-u-ta-tion as child act-ress-es; so did the Den-in Sis-ters, the Kents, the Crisps, and the Deans, while the chil-dren of a pi-o-neer Cin-cin-na-ti act-or, Mr. C. A. Lo-gan, have all be-come known as writ-ers, Ce-lia and Ol-ive Lo-gan be-ing the best known.

But the most a-mus-ing of all the "shows" of those ear-ly days was that of a real-ly gift-ed act-or named Al-ex-an-der Drake. He had what was called a "Flat-boat" the-a-tre; and used to go up and down the O-hi-o Riv-er. When he came to a town or vil-lage he would tie up at the land-ing, and send a man out through the place to tell the coun-try peo-ple that there would be a show that night on the flat-boat. The coun-try peo-ple would come in flocks from far and near; but as mon-ey was scarce in those days, Mr. Drake would let the farm-ers come in-to the show for what-ev-er they chose to bring him—a ham, a pair of chick-ens, a tur-key, a bag of flour, a bas-ket of gro-cer-ies or veg-e-ta-bles, a pair of shoes, a few yards of cal-i-co or cloth. An-y-thing would old Drake take that could be worn or eat-en, for he had a ve-ry large fam-i-ly of sons and daugh-ters to clothe and feed. He had so ma-ny that he did not have to en-gage a-ny act-ors be-sides them, and they were called "The Drake Fam-i-ly."

One even-ing a far-mer drove down to the land-ing with a big load of peo-ple. He had a calf tied to the tail of his wag-on, and this he of-fered as the price of ad-mis-sion for all his friends to the show. Pa-pa Drake took the calf and tied it up, but all through the play it was moo-moo-ing, and the geese cack-led, and hens clucked, and pigs squealed. Would not my lit-tle friends think it ve-ry fun-ny to pay a pair of chick-ens or a lit-tle pig to the cir-cus to get in?

The Drake fam-i-ly al-ways had their fish-ing-lines out o-ver the side of the boat troll-ing for fish, and when they got a bite they would run off the stage and pull in a fish, and the au-di-ence would wait till they got back for the play to go on. One night they were play-ing a piece called "The Stran-ger." In one place The Stran-ger calls "Fran-cis!"—his man-ser-vant. When Fran-cis comes, The Stran-ger says "I called three times—why did you not come?"

Fran-cis in the real play says "I came, sir, when I heard you call;" but one of the Drake boys, who was the Fran-cis on the flat-boat, said when asked "Why did you not come?"

"Be-cause I was pull-ing in the pret-ti-est four-teen-pound cat-fish you ev-er laid eyes on."

One night there was an im-mense au-di-ence on the boat, which some-how got loose from its fas-ten-ings and drift-ed; drift-ed far a-way from the shore. Ev-er-y-one was so in-ter-est-ed in the play that it was not no-ticed that the flat-boat was loose un-til the peo-ple want-ed to go home. Then it was found that they were sev-er-al miles from shore. But no-bod-y mind-ed. There was plen-ty to eat, and Mrs. Drake and her daugh-ters cooked them a big sup-per, and the Drake boys played the fid-dle and the drum, and the act-ors and act-ress-es and the coun-try folks danced to-geth-er, and then had a good time till morn-ing, when the flat-boat was put a-bout and they all got safe home.

At one time were to be found in Cin-cin-na-ti the art-ists James H. Beard and Will-iam H. Pow-ell. In 1840 Thom-as Bu-chan-an Read be-gan his life work here as a sculp-tor. But he soon gave up this branch of art, and gave his time and thoughts to mak-ing pict-ures and writ-ing vers-es, which brought him fame and ma-ny friends.

CHAPTER XXVIII.

THE CIVIL WAR.

FOR years ere the Civ-il War came, the talk of "Slave States" and "Free States" was heard in all parts of our land. O-hi-o was made up, as you know, of men who were born in the South as well as those from New Eng-land; and each felt that those in the land from which he came were in the right. So it was that all the men in the State did not think the same way.

As far back as 1836 the of-fice of the "Phil-an-thro-pist" in Cin-cin-na-ti was sacked by a mob; and in 1841 the mob broke in-to it once more. This pa-per took the part of the poor slaves, and said in strong terms that the South had no right to keep them in their low state. That was why the friends of the slave States looked on the pa-per as a foe of which they would be glad to be rid.

But when the war was a fixed thing, and men both North and South saw that they must fight for what they thought was right, then when our coun-

try's flag was threat-ened, the true spir-it of O-hi-o
showed it-self.   The gold of her rich men was
poured out like wa-ter for the cause of the Un-ion,
and her brave sons were a-mong the first to reach
the scenes of strife.

In 1856 O-hi-o had for her Gov-er-nor Sal-mon
P. Chase, who in time held one of the high-est
plac-es in our land.   By his fore-thought O-hi-o was
much more read-y for the call to arms, when it
sound-ed through the Un-ion, than most of the oth-er
States.   When Mr. Chase had tak-en his seat as the
head of the State, he called the men in pow-er to
him and said: "We must have some sol-diers in
our State, men of our own cit-ies and towns, who
will know how to han-dle a gun, and o-bey an or-der
of war when it is giv-en."   The old folk of the State
could not see the use of this, and looked up-on it as
one of Mr. Chase's strange i-deas; but the young
men were glad to meet and drill, so Gov-er-nor
Chase had but lit-tle trou-ble in form-ing his mi-li-tia,
as such a force of sol-diers is called.

In the old days of In-dian fights each town had
just such a mi-li-tia; but ma-ny years had passed
since then; and the old mus-ter-day was a thing
well nigh for-got-ten; while the guns and swords
which were used at that time were lost or cov-ered
with rust.   O-hi-o was no worse than her sis-ter

States in this; they had seen so much fight-ing west
of the moun-tains that they were glad to rest and
for-get the ills of war. Gov-er-nor Chase was not a

GOV-ER-NOR DEN-NI-SON.

man to give up when once he wished a thing; so in
1859 he went to Day-ton to see the mi-li-tia,—thir-ty
com-pan-ies in all, from ma-ny towns in the State.

In 1860, Will-iam Den-ni-son was made Gov-er-nor of the State of O-hi-o, in the place of Mr. Chase. Though Gov-er-nor Den-ni-son did not know much a-bout troops or things of war, he felt that Mr. Chase did; and so tried to keep things in the same way that Mr. Chase had left them. But he was a fine man, and knew much of bank-ing and rail-roads, and how to make both pay. Folks called him a good gov-er-nor in time of peace, and at last he showed him-self quite as good in time of war.

On that dark morn of A-pril 15, 1861, when the cry of the fall of Sum-ter sent a chill to the hearts of ev-er-y one, Gov-er-nor Den-ni-son sent to the towns through the State for men to save our flag; and ere three days had gone by he had more flock to his call than he knew what to do with. It was but the 18th of A-pril when the First and Sec-ond O-hi-o Reg-i-ments were made out of the com-pan-ies which had hur-ried to Co-lum-bus. They were in most part the mi-li-tia from the towns, and were let-tered in the or-der they reached the ci-ty.

First O-hi-o—Com-pa-ny A, Lan-cas-ter Guards; Com-pa-ny B, La-fay-ette Guards (Day-ton); Com-pa-ny C, Day-ton Light Guards; Com-pa-ny D, Mont-gom-er-y Guards; Com-pa-ny E, Cleve-land Grays; Com-pa-ny F, Hi-ber-ni-an Guards (Cleve-land); Com-pa-ny G, Ports-mouth Guards; Com-pa-ny H, Zanes-ville Guards; Com-pa-ny I, Mans-field Guards; Com-pa-ny K, Jack-son Guards (Ham-il-ton).

Sec-ond O-hi-o—Com-pa-ny A, Ro-ver Guards (Cin-cin-na-ti); Com-pa-ny B, Co-lum-bus Vi-dettes; Com-pa-ny C, Co-lum-bus Fen-ci-bles; Com-pa-ny D, Zou-ave Guards (Cin-cin-na-ti); Com-pa-ny E, La-fay-ette Guards (Cin-cin-na-ti); Com-pa-ny F, Spring-field Zou-aves; Com-pa-ny G, Pick-a-way Com-pa-ny; Com-pa-ny H, Steu-ben-ville Com-pa-ny; Com-pa-ny I, Cov-ing-ton Blues (Mi-a-mi Coun-ty); Com-pa-ny K, Pick-a-way Com-pa-ny.

Some of these men had no guns or clothes fit for war work, but the call from Wash-ing-ton was "send them on at once; we will give them all they need." So in that way the first O-hi-o men rushed to the front. Soon guns and gold to buy all the need-ed things for the men came in as fast as it was need-ed; and reg-i-ment af-ter reg-i-ment marched off to the war.

When in answer to the call of Pres-i-dent Lin-coln for more men, the gov-er-nor of Ken-tuck-y sent the word: "I say em-phat-i-cal-ly that Ken-tuck-y will fur-nish no troops for the wick-ed pur-pose of sub-du-ing her sis-ter South-ern States," was known, Gov-er-nor Den-ni-son said: "If Ken-tuck-y will not fill her quo-ta, O-hi-o will fill it for her!" and he

more than kept his word. In two days two reg-i-
ments were sent off; and be-fore two weeks had
gone by, O-hi-o had sent men e-nough to make up
not on-ly her own share, but that of Ken-tuck-y and
half of Vir-gin-ia.

At the War Of-fice in Wash-ing-ton it was found
that in just six-teen days from the time the Pres-i-
dent called for men, O-hi-o had of-fered 75,000,
which was the whole num-ber the Pres-i-dent had
asked from the whole North. What State did more
than that? This was the first month of the war; for
the next four years 310,000 men left home and
friends in O-hi-o and went to the front. More than
half the men of the State lived on farms, and these
left their lands and flocks in the care of the wo-men
folk when the call came for them to go.

We are apt to pride our-selves up-on the ma-ny
brave gen-er-als O-hi-o gave to the cause; but do not
those who filled these reg-i-ments mer-it quite as
much praise? Old men who could not take part in
the strife, count-ed their sons and sent them forth.
They were at times forced to go to camp and watch
by some dear one as he died of dis-ease or cold,
and then they came back with sad hearts, bring-ing
what was left of the bright youth who marched
a-way un-der the dear old flag a few months be-fore,
to place it in the church-yard near the old home.

A-gain the old man count-ed his sons, and sent oth-ers to take the place of the dead. News came home of fear-ful bat-tles in which loved ones had been killed, or what was oft-times worse, sent to die in the ill-kept pris-ons. Ev-er-y home had some loved one miss-ing; but the O-hi-o heart, brave and strong, on-ly worked with great-er zeal for the cause which to them was a Ho-ly one. They were sure that God, in His good time, would give them the vic-to-ry. In the mean-time the rich men cared for the poor wo-men and chil-dren left at home; and so, if too old to fight, gave their mite to the cause of the Un-ion.

CHAPTER XXIX.

OHIO GENERALS.

In war, as in most oth-er things, some men must take the lead; so when O-hi-o was called on for her men best fit-ted to lead in the sud-den war which had come to us, two were at once named. A few weeks lat-er these were both raised to the high-est plac-es in the ar-my. One was made a Ma-jor-Gen-er-al, and the oth-er a Brig-a-dier in the reg-u-lar ar-my, though be-fore this the first had been a sim-ple Cap-tain, and the oth-er a Lieu-ten-ant.

George B. Mc-Clel-lan, the first of these, was the first Gen-er-al sent by O-hi-o when the war broke out. He was born in Phil-a-del-phi-a, De-cem-ber 3, 1826. His fath-er, a doc-tor of note, had his son well taught; and when George was six-teen years old he was sent to West Point. He fin-ished his term there just as the war with Mex-i-co broke out,

and at once was sent to the scene of strife. In time he was made Cap-tain; and when the war was done Mr. Jef-fer-son Da-vis, then Sec-re-ta-ry of War, sent him to Eu-rope to learn what he could of the fight which was at the time rag-ing in the Cri-me-a.

In 1857 Cap-tain Mc-Clel-lan left the ar-my, and in a short time was made pres-i-dent of a rail-road in

G. B. Mc CLEL-LAN.

O-hi-o; so it was he came to live at Cin-cin-na-ti, and was called an O-hi-o Gen-er-al.

When the war broke out, Gov-er-nor Den-ni-son looked a-bout for a man to help him or-gan-ize his troops, and Mc-Clel-lan was point-ed out as a West Point man, and one well fit-ted for the task; so the Gov-er-nor sent for him to come to the Cap-i-tol. But by the time Gov-er-nor Den-ni-son thought to have his help, Mc-Clel-lan was called to be Ma-jor-Gen-er-al, and to com-mand the troops of O-hi-o, In-di-an-a, and Il-li-nois.

Af-ter the bat-tle of Bull Run, Gen-er-al Mc-Clel-lan was giv-en charge of the ar-my of the Po-to-mac. At this time, this branch of our for-ces was in a bad state, and the men at the North felt that some-thing ought to be done be-fore they could ex-pect much good to come from its bat-tles. Mc-Clel-lan at once set to work to re-or-gan-ize it; and ere long had the pleas-ure of see-ing it the best drilled bod-y of men we had. The skill which he showed in this work was praised by men in all parts of the land.

In 1864, his name was raised a-gainst Mr. Lin-coln's for Pres-i-dent of the U-nit-ed States, but he had on-ly a few votes.

Be-fore this, some trou-ble a-bout war mat-ters caused him to give up his place as head of the troops; and now he went to Eu-rope, where he lived with his fam-i-ly till long af-ter the close of the war.

The oth-er man who was named as a fit lead-er was Wil-liam Starke Rose-crans. That name is Ger-man, and means "a wreath of ros-es,"—is-n't it a pret-ty one? The own-er of it was born in Kings-ton, Del-a-ware Coun-ty, O-hi-o, Sep-tem-ber 6, 1819. He was a bright, stu-di-ous boy, and at fif-teen was mas-ter of all that the school in his dis-trict could teach. He was a good boy as well, and was e-ven at that ear-ly age fond of re-li-gion, and ev-er read-y to talk and ar-gue up-on the theme.

In his class at West Point were fif-ty-six boys, and young Rose-crans ranked fifth a-mong them all.

When the cry of war was raised, Rose-crans was quick to o-bey it, and from the first did all in his

WIL-LIAM S. ROSE-CRANS.

pow-er to save our coun-try's hon-or. He chose the sites, and fit-ted up both Camp Den-ni-son, near Cin-cin-na-ti, and Camp Chase, at Co-lum-bus; while o-ver the lat-ter he had com-mand. Then he went to West Vir-gin-ia, where it is said he was so bus-y that he was sel-dom out of his sad-dle, and took his meals on his horse quite as of-ten as at his ta-ble. He won some great bat-tles, and by all was known to be a great gen-er-al and brave sol-dier.

CHAPTER XXX.

ULYSSES SIMPSON GRANT.

As Vir-gin-ia is said to be the "Moth-er of Pres-i-dents," so in truth could O-hi-o be called the "Moth-er of Gen-er-als." Strange as it may seem, the on-ly real "Gen-er-als" our land has ev-er had were all born in O-hi-o. There are but three of these, on-ly one of whom is liv-ing. They were U-lys-ses S. Grant, who was the first raised to the of-fice, Gen-er-al Sher-man, and Gen-er-al Sher-i-dan.

Way back in Wash-ing-ton's time, when a war with France seemed a sure thing, Wash-ing-ton was made a Lieu-ten-ant-Gen-er-al, a grade that none in the Rev-o-lu-tion-a-ry war had reached; but as no war came he did not hold the of-fice in the field. In the war with Mex-i-co, Gen-er-al Scott, who won much praise from ev-er-y-one by the quick way in which he brought peace a-bout, was raised by Con-gress to the same grade. It was for U-lys-ses S. Grant, though, to win the rank,—first of Lieu-ten-ant-Gen-er-al, and then, as a last grand step, that of Gen-er-al.

Hi-ram U-lys-ses Grant, since called U-lys-ses

Simp-son Grant, was born on the 27th of A-pril, 1822, in a lit-tle one-sto-ry house on the banks of the O-hi-o, at the town of Point Pleas-ant, in Cler-mont Coun-ty.   His fath-er was a poor tan-ner, and could

send his son to school but three months in the year; yet when this son went to West Point on Ju-ly 1, 1839, he stood well in his class.   Like Mc-Clel-lan, he fought in the war with Mex-i-co, and was said to be a brave young of-fi-cer; but it was for the war of the Re-bel-lion to show what the man was made of. In the first months of the war we heard but lit-tle of him; but lat-er, when bat-tle af-ter bat-tle was fought un-der Gen-er-al Grant, and vic-to-ry was ev-er his, e-nough could not be said in his praise. He was a qui-et, mod-est man, and nev-er went out of the path he thought the right one, to gain an-y good for him-self. Hon-ors were show-ered up-on him, and he was pleased with them; but the i-dea nev-er seemed to come to him that he could go out of his way to seek them.

In 1869 U-lys-ses S. Grant be-came pres-i-dent of the U-nit-ed States, which of-fice he held to March 4, 1877,—two terms. The next year he went to Eu-rope. In 1879 he came home to A-mer-i-ca, hav-ing made a tour round the world since he left home. He died in Ju-ly, 1886, much mourned by the whole land.

CHAPTER XXXI.

THE TWO OTHER GENERALS.

In 1815 there came to Lan-cas-ter a wid-ow with her sons, one of which soon be-came a fine law-yer, and in time a judge. He took a wife while a ve-ry young man, and in 1829 died, leav-ing a wid-ow with e-lev-en chil-dren to care for. Of these, two have since be-come known through-out the world. The eighth of them, a lad of six or sev-en, was John

Sher-man, since re-pre-sen-ta-tive and sen-a-tor in con-gress; and the sixth, then nine years of age, a bright-eyed, red-haired, play-lov-ing ur-chin, was Wil-liam Te-cum-seh Sher-man.

Up to the time of the death of his fath-er, Te-cum-seh Sher-man lived a hap-py, ac-tive, out-of-door life with his sis-ters and broth-ers; but when death took the judge, the moth-er did not see her way clear to bring up her large fam-i-ly as she wished. At this time Thom-as Ew-ing, a law-yer and friend of the late judge, wished to a-dopt one of the boys. "I must have the smart-est of them," Mr. Ew-ing said to the wid-ow when he of-fered to take a boy. And it is said that when the moth-er and old-est sis-ter had talked the mat-ter o-ver, they a-greed that "Cump," just then slid-ing down a sand-bank back of the house, was the one to go.

Mr. Ew-ing has since said that he was the best boy to do an er-rand he ev-er knew, and that he was ev-er hon-est, faith-ful, and re-li-a-ble. What praise could be great-er than that?

He fin-ished at West Point in 1840. When the war came it found Sher-man rea-dy, and a brave fight he made through the whole strife; but he is best known, and will ev-er be re-mem-bered, by his won-der-ful "march to the sea," which has al-ways been called one of the great-est feats of the war.

Gen-er-al Sher-man is the on-ly one of the three "real Gen-er-als" who still lives, and I am sure all his boy and girl friends who read this will wish that ma-ny years of life may still be his. If you should ev-er have a chance to look up-on his kind-ly face, think as you look at him that you see one of the brav-est men A-mer-i-ca ev-er held.

E-lev-en years af-ter Wil-liam Te-cum-seh Sher-man first saw the light, and but a doz-en miles from his home, a lit-tle I-rish ba-by was born, and a few days la-ter, chris-tened in the vil-lage Church of St. Jo-seph, as the Cath-o-lic church of Som-er-set was called.

In due time the ba-by grew to be a lad, and was sent to the vil-lage school, which was taught by an I-rish teach-er who thought no boy could be hap-py or good if they did

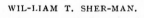

WIL-LIAM T. SHER-MAN.

not have a fre-quent taste of the birch. This wise teach-er was called Pat-rick Mc-Nan-ly, and, as can be guessed, was not much liked by the boys.

One ter-ri-bly cold morn of 1842 or 1843, two of Pat-rick's schol-ars reached the school-house a lit-tle be-fore time. They crawled in through the win-dow to get warmed, and when once in, found a pail-ful of ice-wa-ter in the room. Now, like some oth-er boys we all know, these two were full of fun; and the ab-sence of work, and sight of the ice-wa-ter, caused them to play a trick up-on the teach-er. They fixed the pail o-ver the door in such a man-ner that the o-pen-ing of the door would tilt it up-on the head of the one com-ing in, and then hid in a hay-mow near by to see the fun.

Pat-rick came trot-ting a-long, rub-bing his hands to keep them warm, raised the latch, and bolt-ed in, —just as the pail turned o-ver his head. It is safe to say he did-n't feel kind-ly to-ward a-ny one just then; but not a boy was to be seen. He looked all a-round, in-side and out, but no one was in sight. So, arm-ing him-self with a six-foot hick-o-ry stick, he sat by the stove to dry, and to watch for the first boy who came.

A lit-tle fel-low soon came; but the mo-ment his hand was up-on the latch Pat-rick had him by the col-lar, and shook him fierce-ly, to "shake the truth out of him," he said. The as-ton-ished looks and loud yells of the lad showed Pat-rick he had not found the right one. As each came in, he had the same treat-ment, and in time the two in the hay-mow climbed down, got their shak-ing, and went to their seats.

It chanced that Phil Sher-i-dan was late that morn-ing, and as each had proved he knew noth-ing

of the af-fair, the last must be the guil-ty one. So
as he o-pened the door Pat-rick made a dive for him;
Phil dodged and ran. Pat-rick thought that was a
sure proof he had found the right one, so he set
chase. A-way went Phil up the street, and a-way
went the teach-er af-ter him, bare-head-ed, stick in
hand, the whole school bring-ing up the rear, all on
the run.

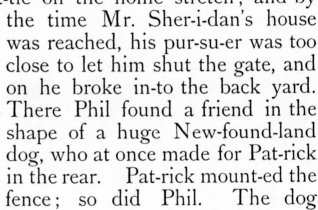

Phil lost a lit-tle on the home stretch; and by
the time Mr. Sher-i-dan's house
was reached, his pur-su-er was too
close to let him shut the gate, and
on he broke in-to the back yard.
There Phil found a friend in the
shape of a huge New-found-land
dog, who at once made for Pat-rick
in the rear. Pat-rick mount-ed the
fence; so did Phil. The dog
snapped at Pat-rick's heels, and he thought it best to
climb an ap-ple tree near at hand.

PHIL SHER-I-DAN.

"Take a-way your"—and here he used a bad
word, I am sor-ry to say—"dog, Phil," said he, "or
I'll bate the life out of ye!"

"Like to see you!" said Phil; "watch him,
Ro-ver!" and with that he got an old piece of car-
pet and laid it un-der the tree for the dog to watch
o-ver.

The dog lay down on it, and Phil mount-ed the fence, where he sat eye-ing his foe, with his chin in his hands and his el-bows on his knees. "What do you want to lick me for?" asked Phil.

"What did you throw the wa-ther on me for?" was the an-swer.

"I did-n't throw an-y wa-ter on you."

"Ye did, though, be-kase none of the oth-er boys did, and I'll pol-ish you to death in-tire-ly, if ye don't let me down." He start-ed down, but Ro-ver made for his foot, and the teach-er made up the tree a-gain, call-ing for Phil's fa-ther.

The noise brought Mr. Sher-i-dan to the door; and great was his sur-prise to find his son with the rest of the school on the fence, and the teach-er up an ap-ple tree watched o-ver by a dog.

"What are you do-ing up in that ap-ple tree, McNan-ly?" asked Mr. Sher-i-dan.

"Ah, that div-il-ish boy of yours, Mis-ther Sher-i-dan, will be the death of me yet. It's all his do-ings, sir. He poored a whole buck-et of wa-ther on me this morn-in', and whin I want-ed to give him a da-cent rip-ri-mand, he ran a-way; and for the sake of the dis-ci-pline of the school, I went to catch him, and he got that big baste of yours af-ther me, and I had to climb the tree to de-find me-self!"

"I did-n't throw a-ny wa-ter at all," says Phil;

"all I know a-bout it is that he went to whip-ping me this morn-ing be-fore I got in."

Mr. Sher-i-dan said it might be well to let the case go for a while, but the teach-er had his rep-u-ta-tion at stake, and would not a-gree to that. Then Mr. Sher-i-dan called the dog off, but Ro-ver looked at Phil and would-n't stir.

"Take that div-il-ish dog a-way, or I'll bate the life out of ye both in-tire-ly!" called the i-rate Pat-rick.

"Bet-ter come down first," Phil sug-gest-ed; "watch him, Ro-ver!—but I'll tell you what I'll do," he add-ed af-ter a pause; "if you won't whip me I'll call him off. He won't go if fath-er calls all day— be-sides, he sees you're im-pos-ing on me."

Pat-rick ar-gued and plead-ed, but the terms were not changed. The hot race and the cold wa-ter had giv-en him a dread-ful chill, so with teeth chat-ter-ing he at last made the prom-ise.

"I'll tell you what, Phil," said he; "if you'll just call off that baste, I'll not bate you this time, in-dade I won't."

"Why did-n't you say so at first?" said Phil. "Come a-way, Ro-ver." And a-way Ro-ver did come, and a-way the teach-er came, al-most too much chilled to climb down the tree.

This was the first sur-ren-der to Phil-ip Sher-i-dan. Phil said the teach-er kept his word that time, but he put two flog-gings in-to ev-er-y one he gave him af-ter that.

That bright boy came in time to be the third full "Gen-er-al" in our land, and his war rec-ord was a brave and grand one. It was on-ly a few weeks a-go that the coun-try mourned his death, which took place on Au-gust 5, 1888.

CHAPTER XXXII.

GENERALS WHO DID NOT SEE THE END.

At one time there lived in the north part of O-hi-o a poor black-smith named Mc-Pher-son. He had tak-en land for a farm, and worked ear-ly and late in clear-ing it of trees, while dur-ing the day he plied his trade for the neigh-bors near. To him was born a son on the 14th of No-vem-ber, 1828, whom he named James Birds-eye. The boy was a good har-dy lad, who in time was taught to pick brush, drive the horse, and by and by to plough and chop wood.

When James was thir-teen years old, his fath-er's health gave way, and the wife was forced to sup-port the fam-i-ly. James wished to help her, and a chance came for him to work in a gro-cer-y store a few miles a-way; so with a heav-y heart he left the dear old home, and be-came first a store-boy, and then a clerk, for Mr. Rob-ert Smith, of Green Spring. Af-ter store hours he read good books, and at last was sent to West Point by kind friends, where at one time he was in the class with Phil Sher-i-dan.

Like the oth-er West Point men, when the war broke out Mc-Pher-son went to the front; and was so brave and bright that no doubt he would have gained great re-nown had his life been spared. On the eve of a grand vic-to-ry he was shot down, and died on the spot. Ma-ny hearts were made sad by the death of the no-ble young man, and O-hi-o has ev-er held his name in af-fec-tion-ate es-teem.

Ma-jor-Gen-er-al Orms-by Mc-Knight Mit-chel was an-oth-er O-hi-o man who died be-fore the war was done. Though born in Ken-tuck-y, Gen-er-al Mit-chel came to O-hi-o when on-ly four years old.

So bright was the boy that be-fore he was nine years of age he was read-ing Vir-gil. At twelve he was thought to be old e-nough to earn his liv-ing, so was put in a coun-try store as er-rand boy and clerk.

He worked for twen-ty-five cents a week, and not on-ly tend-ed the store, but cut wood, made fires, scrubbed and scoured the floors, and fetched wa-ter

for the house.   But the boy who read Lat-in and
knew some-thing of Greek verbs be-fore he was
twelve was sure to rise in the world; and be-fore he
was fif-teen young Mit-chel start-ed for West Point.

GEN-ER-AL MIT-CHEL.

He was ver-y poor, and had to walk part of the way;
but at last he reached the school, with his knap-sack
on his back and twen-ty-five cents in his pock-et.

Though un-der the age when boys were us-u-al-ly ad-mit-ted, he passed as well as the old-er boys in the class.

When his West Point life was o-ver, he stud-ied law; and when on-ly twen-ty-three years old went to Cin-cin-na-ti, where he had for a part-ner a man whose name has since be-come high-ly re-nowned in all O-hi-o. It was Ed-ward D. Mans-field.

In 1834 he was made a pro-fes-sor in the "Col-lege of Cin-cin-na-ti." He loved to view the stars at night, and knew more a-bout them than an-y one else in the West. At last he urged the O-hi-o men to build a great build-ing and place in it a fine tel-e-scope worth ma-ny thou-sand dol-lars. Nich-o-las Long-worth gave a great piece of ground on a hill-top near the ci-ty for the ob-ser-va-to-ry, as the build-ing was called.

Here Mr. Mit-chel worked till the war came, when he once more took up the life of a sol-dier. But he did not do much fight-ing, for on the 30th of Oc-to-ber, 1862, he died of yel-low fe-ver.

CHAPTER XXXIII.

OTHER BRAVE GENERALS.

MA-JOR-GEN-ER-AL IR-VING MC-DOW-ELL was one of O-hi-o's gen-er-als; and though he lost two great bat-tles, he was brave and bright, and is said to have been one of the best mil-i-ta-ry schol-ars in the ar-my.

GEN-ER-AL Mc-DOW-ELL.

He was born in the vil-lage of Frank-lin-ton, on the 15th of Oc-to-ber, 1818.

Don Car-los Bu-ell, also one of the best mil-i-ta-ry schol-ars in our land and was the he-ro of some of the great-est and first bat-tles of the war. He was born near Mar-i-et-ta, on the 23d of March, 1818. His fath-er died when Don Car-los was a small boy, and the lad was tak-en to live with his un-cle in Law-rence-burg, In-di-an-a. He was a qui-et boy, but when roused was a brave, and ev-en sav-age, fight-er. It is said that soon af-ter he reached his new home the "town bul-ly" a-mong the lads at that time thought he would see of what stuff the "new boy" was made. They met at the town pump one morn-ing, a ring was formed, and the new boy proved his met-tle by beat-ing the bul-ly.

He was one of the class of 1841 at West Point; and when the war came worked hard for the Un-ion. Gen-er-al Bu-ell is one of the few Gen-er-als who still live.

GEN-ER-AL BU-ELL.

Quin-cy Ad-ams Gill-more was born at Black Riv-er, O-hi-o, on Feb-ru-a-ry 28, 1825. His fath-er was a Mass-a-chu-setts man, and fond of the Ad-ams par-ty. The news of the e-lec-tion of Mr. Ad-ams as Pres-i-dent reached his vil-lage on the day his son was born, so the twice hap-py man said his son should bear the name of a Pres-i-dent, and at once called him Quin-cy Ad-ams.

Young Gill-more was a bright schol-ar, and by the time he was four-teen had learned all the coun-try school could teach.   It is said that a po-em of

his gained for him the chance to en-ter West Point. A man from his place was in Con-gress and had a chance to send some boy friend to that school. He tried two or three, but in each case the boy for some cause could not go. At last he asked the ed-i-tor of the pa-per of the town who he thought would be the one to send.

GEN-ER-AL GILL-MORE.

"Have you seen the po-em by the young grad-u-ate of the E-ly-ri-a High School?" asked he.   This pleased Mr. Ham-lin, and he sent to the boy who wrote "E-rie" and asked him if he would like to go to West Point.

Quin-cy thought a few min-utes, and then an-swered that he would.

He had start-ed to stud-y for a doc-tor, and when his pa-rents heard that he had giv-en up such high hopes for a sol-dier's life, they were not well pleased. He was forced to ask his fath-er for mon-ey to take him East, and to buy the few things he need-ed; and his fath-er said in re-ply: " I will give it to you, if you will prom-ise to come out at the head of your class."

At the end of the first year Ca-det Gill-more was fourth; but at the end of the course he had kept his prom-ise, and did "come out at the head of the class." In the war he was no-ted for his brave acts, and the skill with which he planned and made forts which held the foe at bay.

It was but a few months a-go that the coun-try was called up-on to mourn his death.

In-to the of-fice of the *Lew-is-burg Dem-o-crat,* then ed-i-ted by Judge George R. Bar-rett, there came some time in the year 1833 a poor boy of a-bout fif-teen years of age. His pa-rents were un-a-ble to send him to a good school, and he had grown up with but lit-tle book learn-ing.

He was a bright, act-ive lad, and the print-ing of-fice proved to be the best of schools for him. In fact, he learned so fast that at the end of two years he could do a man's work ; and so as a chance came up, he left the news-pa-per and took charge of a gang of men on some pub-lic work. A-gain he suc-ceed-ed; and a-bout this time he moved to O-hi-o, bought a print-ing of-fice at De-fi-ance, and pub-lished the *North-west-ern Dem-o-crat.* Then he took a large con-tract of rail-road to build and made some gold by it. But he kept on with his pa-per, which in time be-came a pow-er in his State.

This man was James B. Steed-man, who was born in North-um-ber-land Coun-ty, Penn-syl-va-ni-a, on the 30th of Ju-ly, 1818.

In 1861 Mr. Steed-man, who then lived in To-le-do, was one of the first to send to Gov-er-nor Den-ni-son the of-fer of a reg-i-ment. This was the Four-teenth O-hi-o, which in nine days af-ter the fall of Sum-ter was fit-ted out and read-y for work. Gen-er-al Steed-man was brave, bold, and hear-ty in his ways, be-loved by his troops and ma-ny friends, and did much hard fight-ing for his coun-try.

On the 27th day of Sep-tem-ber, 1830, at West Hart-ford, Ver-mont, was born a child who in time was named Wil-liam Bab-cock Ha-zen. He came from good New Eng-land stock, and his grand-fath-er had fought at both Lex-ing-ton and Bun-ker Hill. When the boy was three years of age, his fath-er moved to Hu-ron, O-hi-o, and set-tled up-on a farm, on which some of his fam-i-ly still live.

In time the fu-ture Gen-er-al was sent to West Point, from which place he grad-u-at-ed in 1855.

He then went to the Pa-cif-ic coast, and served in the In-dian war, which at that time was rag-ing in Or-e-gon. From that time up to the win-ter of 1859 Lieu-ten-ant Ha-zen was in fights with the In-dians. In No-vem-ber of that year, while in a hand-to-hand com-bat with a Co-man-che In-dian, he re-ceived se-vere wounds in

GEN-ER-AL HA-ZEN.

the hand and side, which made him ill for a long time.

But like the oth-er brave sons of O-hi-o, when the call to war came he was read-y and glad to o-bey it. Through the war he fought brave-ly and well, and so long as the bat-tles at Stone Knob, Mis-sion Ridge, At-lan-ta, and Fort Mc-Al-lis-ter are re-mem-bered, the name of Gen-er-al Ha-zen will be cher-ished and loved.

Since the war, Gen-er-al Ha-zen has been at the head of those who fore-tell the wea-ther, and warn the land of storms and cold.

CHAPTER XXXIV.

OTHER BRAVE GENERALS—(Continued).

Rob-ert Cum-ming Schenck, who was sent to Con-gress, and a-cross the sea as a For-eign Min-is-ter be-fore the war, was one of our brav-est and a-blest gen-er-als, and since the war was a-gain sent a-cross the sea as Min-is-ter to Eng-land. He was born in the town of Frank-lin, O-hi-o, on the 4th of Oc-to-ber, 1809.

His fath-er, Gen-er-al Will-iam C. Schenck, an ear-ly set-tler in the Mi-am-i Val-ley, was a brave of-fi-cer in the North-west-ern ar-my un-der Gen-er-al Har-ri-son; but he died when his son Rob-ert was but twelve years of age. When he was fif-teen, he was so bright that he en-tered the Soph-o-more Class at Mi-am-i U-ni-ver-si-ty, Ox-ford, O-hi-o, and grad-

GEN-ER-AL SCHENCK.

u-at-ed in 1827. He stayed at Ox-ford for the next
three years as tu-tor of French and Lat-in. Then
he stud-ied law, and as in all else, was in a few years
a ve-ry suc-cess-ful law-yer.

When the at-tack was made on Fort Sum-ter,
Mr. Schenck at once of-fered him-self as a sol-dier to
Pres-i-dent Lin-coln, and was made Brig-a-di-er-Gen-
er-al of Vol-un-teers. He was both wise and brave,
and fought side by side with his men.

In the sec-ond bat-tle of Bull Run, while urg-ing
his men for-ward in the thick-est of the fight, Gen-
er-al Schenck was bad-ly wound-ed and tak-en from
the field. But the men who were near him at the
time de-light in tell-ing of the rage the wound-ed
man was in at the loss of his sword. It had been in
his hand at the mo-ment the ball struck his wrist,
and was thrown some dis-tance a-way. The place
he was in was near, and in full sight of, the en-e-my;
and his staff, fear-ing he would be killed, tried to
hur-ry him a-way. It was of no use; the Gen-er-al
would not move, no mat-ter how hard they urged,
till the sword was found; then he was tak-en to the
hos-pi-tal, and his wound dressed. For a long time
he suf-fered from it, and his arm was so bad-ly hurt,
that he has nev-er since been a-ble to write with it.

The loss of the use of Gen-er-al Schenck's right
hand was a loss to the whole North, for his clear

head and brave heart were sad-ly need-ed at the time.

With him, on his staff, he had a num-ber of a-ble men who were bet-ter fit-ted to take the charge of af-fairs than some high-er of-fi-cers. A-mong these was Colo-nel Donn Pi-att, who is now known to us as a man of let-ters on-ly, but who in those days showed him-self quite as well fit-ted for a lead-er on the field of strife.

At one time, just be-fore Lee's ar-my en-tered Penn-syl-va-ni-a, Colo-nel Pi-att was sent to Win-ches-ter to take ob-ser-va-tions. See-ing dan-ger for our men, he or-dered Gen-er-al Rob-ert H. Mil-roy to leave the place and fall back to Har-per's Fer-ry; and had he been o-beyed a sad fight would have been saved. But Gen-er-al Hal-leck told Mil-roy to stay where he was; and in three days the en-e-my came, and sur-round-ed the troops, so that the poor Gen-er-al and his men were forced to cut their way through the Reb-el line, with a loss of 2,300 pris-on-ers.

CHAPTER XXXV.

THE SIEGE OF CINCINNATI.

In the ear-ly days of 1862 a new name was heard with fear by folk on the banks of the O-hi-o. The Un-ion men in Ken-tuck-y were set up-on by a troop of dar-ing men, their cat-tle and hors-es tak-en, and homes burned. One day word would come from one place, and the next from an-oth-er some dis-tance a-way, of the hav-oc done by this band, until the whole re-gion was in con-stant dread of John Mor-gan's Ken-tuck-y Cav-al-ry, as the troop was called.

The lead-er of this band was a na-tive of Hunts-ville, Al-a-ba-ma, but since he was a small boy he had lived in Ken-tuck-y. He had grown up in the free and ea-sy life of a slave-hold-ing far-mer's son in the heart of that part of Ken-tuck-y known as the " Blue Grass coun-try," went to the Mex-i-can war when but nine-teen, and had lived a bold, free life since then.

He had ma-ny friends a-mong the wild young men of the State, and these went with him to war. Ear-ly in Ju-ly word came to Cin-cin-na-ti, that Mor-gan was on his way to Lou-is-ville ; then a-gain to

Lex-ing-ton. Next came a call for troops from Cin-cin-na-ti to de-fend these ci-ties. A large bo-dy of troops was soon raised and sent to them, and much fear was felt through-out the south part of O-hi-o. At last, to make mat-ters worse, trou-bles broke out be-tween the I-rish and ne-groes of the ci-ty. Hous-es were fired, and for a time a ri-ot of some size was feared.

In Sep-tem-ber the head men in Cin-cin-na-ti were made to feel that on-ly the O-hi-o Riv-er ran be-tween her great store-hous-es and the reb-el ar-my; and at once means were ta-ken to guard the Queen Ci-ty. Lew Wal-lace, a dash-ing young of-fi-cer of vol-un-teers from In-di-an-a, was sent to take com-mand and de-fend the town.

The next morn-ing af-ter he reached the place, and be-fore it was known that the Reb-els were on their way to the ci-ty, men read in their dai-ly pa-pers at their break-fast ta-bles the or-der that all busi-ness must be closed at nine o'clock, and that all the men must meet by 10 A.M. to a-wait or-ders for work; that the fer-ry-boats must not cross the riv-er. The men of the ci-ty were to build breast-works and ri-fle-pits, while the sol-diers from Camp Chase were to fight.

All Cin-cin-na-ti cheer-ful-ly o-beyed this or-der; and had a stran-ger looked in up-on her they would have thought a grand hol-i-day was be-ing held. It

was this prompt work of Gen-er-al Wal-lace which
saved the Queen Ci-ty.

This bright young of-fi-cer was of-ten heard from

GEN-ER-AL LEW WAL-LACE.

dur-ing the war, and now that the war is past,
he has changed his sword for the pen, and the

world knows him as the tal-ent-ed au-thor of "Ben-Hur."

George A. Cus-ter, one of the young-est of O-hi-o's gen-er-als, was born at New Rum-ley, Har-ri-son Coun-ty, O-hi-o, on the 5th of De-cem-ber, 1839. He grad-u-at-ed at West Point in June,

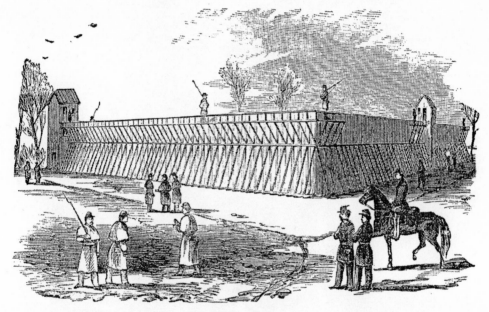

CAMP CHASE.

1861; and leav-ing there on the 18th of Ju-ly, he re-port-ed to Gen-er-al Scott on the 20th, the day be-fore the bat-tle of Bull Run.

The Gen-er-al gave him the choice of be-ing on his staff, or of join-ing his com-pa-ny, then un-der Gen-er-al Mc-Dow-ell, near Cen-tre-ville. Long-ing to see a real fight, the brave young of-fi-cer chose the lat-ter; and af-ter rid-ing all night a-lone, he reached Gen-er-al Mc-Dow-ell's head-quar-ters a-bout three o'clock on the morn-ing of the 21st.

GEN-ER-AL CUS-TER.

All were rea-dy for bat-tle; in fact, it had be-gun ere Lieu-ten-ant Cus-ter had eat-en his has-ty break-fast, giv-en up Gen-er-al Scott's mes-sage, and joined his com-pa-ny.

This was one of the last to leave the field, which it did in good or-der. He served with this com-pa-ny near Wash-ing-ton un-til he was made one of the la-ment-ed Gen-er-al Phil Kear-ney's staff.

Since the war Gen-er-al Cus-ter was sent to fight the In-dians in the far West, and here he lost his life while try-ing to keep in check these mis-er-a-ble sav-ag-es.

CHAPTER XXXVI.

PRESIDENTS FROM OHIO.

OF all the Pres-i-dents of the U-nit-ed States, four have come from O-hi-o. The first of these, Will-liam Hen-ry Har-ri-son, was ninth in or-der from Wash-ing-ton. He was the son of Gov-er-nor Ben-ja-min Har-ri-son, and was born at Berke-ley, Vir-gin-ia, Feb-ru-a-ry 9, 1773.

In 1797, when on-ly twen-ty and four years old, Will-iam H. Har-ri-son was made cap-tain of the North-west Ter-ri-to-ry, and as you have learned, was wise in his deal-ings with the In-dians. When the In-dian fights were o-ver, he was sent to Con-gress from Cin-cin-na-ti. Then he helped to make

FISH-ING IN O-HI-O IN 1800.

the laws of O-hi-o, and in time was sent as Min-is-ter to a foreign land.

In 1840 Gen-er-al Har-ri-son was called to be Pres-i-dent of the U-nit-ed States, and it was this cam-paign which is of-ten spok-en of as the "Sing-ing Cam-paign." In it ma-ny new songs were made and sung by men all o-ver the land. In one of them the fa-mous "Tip-pe-ca-noe and Ty-ler too," was of-ten re-peated. The "Tip-pe-ca-noe," re-fer-ring to a bat-tle in which Gen-er-al Har-ri-son gained a great vic-to-ry, and the "Ty-ler" to the man who was chos-en to be Vice-Pres-i-dent, but who, from the ear-ly death of Mr. Har-ri-son, was Pres-i-dent of our land for nearly four years.

Pres-i-dent Har-ri-son died A-pril 4, 1841, just a month af-ter his in-aug-u-ra-tion.

In 1869 Gen-er-al Grant was made Pres-i-dent of our coun-try. You know what a brave gen-er-al he was, and may be sure that when called to the high-est of-fice in our land he was be-loved and es-teemed by a large part of our peo-ple. So it was not strange that he was chos-en to be Pres-i-dent for an-oth-er four years when his first term was at an end.

No Pres-i-dent has ev-er held his of-fice for three terms, so at the end of eight years General Grant's friends were forced to let him go back to pri-vate life once more. Then it was he made a tour of the world, and was treat-ed as a prince might have been in most of the lands he vis-it-ed.

His death was a sad and hard one, and he fought brave-ly for the life he felt was leav-ing him. At last the end came on Thurs-day, Ju-ly 23d, at 8 A.M. The men of our land felt ve-ry sad when they knew their brave Gen-er-al was no more. And in mem-o-ry of his deeds, on Au-gust 8th, they had the great-est fu-ner-al o-ver his bod-y which New York has ev-er known.

Af-ter this it was tak-en to a tomb pre-pared for it at Riv-er-side Park, on the North Riv-er. This last rest-ing-place is nice-ly cared for, and is dai-ly vis-it-ed by ma-ny stran-gers in the ci-ty, both from this coun-try and those a-cross the sea.

In 1865 Ma-jor-Gen-er-al Ruth-er-ford B. Hayes was made Pres-i-dent, and held his of-fice for one term, that is, for four years.

R. B. Hayes was born at Del-a-ware, O-hi-o, Oc-to-ber 4, 1822. When he grew to be a man he stud-ied law, and in time be-came one of the best law-yers in Cin-cin-na-ti. When the war be-gan, at the first call for men, he left his law of-fice and gave him-self for a sol-dier. He was made ma-jor of the Twen-ty-third O-hi-o In-fan-try on the 7th of June, 1861, and dur-ing the sum-mer of that year he served un-der Gen-er-al Rose-crans in West Vir-gin-ia. In the fall he was pro-mot-ed, and in time be-came Colo-nel, when he was placed in com-mand of the First Brig-ade of the Ka-na-wha di-vi-sion, a po-si-tion he held un-til Sher-i-dan's vic-to-ry at Win-ches-ter, in Sep-tem-ber, 1864. Then he took com-mand of the whole di-vi-sion, and led it till the end of the year.

In this bat-tle of Win-ches-ter, Colo-nel Hayes was at one time lead-ing his men in a charge, when they came sud-den-ly up-on a mo-rass some six-ty yards wide. The wa-ter was knee deep, and in some plac-es cov-ered with hea-vy moss, al-most strong e-nough to bear the weight of a man, while the bot-tom was soft and mi-ry. When the men came to this they stopped, as it did not seem to them that they could cross it; but not so with Colo-nel Hayes. He at once drove his horse in-to the slough; when half way a-cross the poor

an-i-mal stuck fast in the mud and could not move.
Then the Col-o-nel jumped from his back and wad-ed
on, be-ing the first man a-cross. All through the
fight, he stayed near his men, shar-ing their dan-gers
with them, in one of the worst plac-es in the field.

Dur-ing the war he had three hors-es shot from
un-der him, and was wound-ed four times; once
ve-ry bad-ly. When the war was o-ver, Gen-er-al
Hayes was made Ma-jor-Gen-er-al for his brave
deeds dur-ing the last years of strife. Just be-fore
the end came, the men of Cin-cin-na-ti vo-ted to
send him to Con-gress, and in a few years he be-
came Gov-er-nor of O-hi-o.

On the 5th of March, 1877, Mr. Hayes was
in-aug-u-rat-ed Pres-i-dent of the U-nit-ed States.
When his term of of-fice was at an end, he went to
live at Fre-mont, O-hi-o. His wife, Lu-cy Ware
Webb Hayes, who be-fore her mar-riage lived at
Chil-li-coth-e, made ma-ny friends a-mong the tem-
per-ance peo-ple all o-ver the land, while at the
White House, by her brave de-fence of the cause.

Dur-ing the four years in which she held the place
of first la-dy in our land, she nev-er would al-low
wine at her ta-ble; this was a firm stand that no
oth-er la-dy in her po-si-tion had ev-er cared or
dared to take, and it brought her some en-e-mies, as
well as a host of friends.

Mr. and Mrs. Hayes are still in our midst, and Mr. Hayes en-joys the dis-tinc-tion of be-ing the on-ly Ex-Pres-i-dent liv-ing. That he may long con-tin-ue to live is the ear-nest wish of ev-er-y loy-al heart.

On No-vem-ber 19, 1831, at Or-ange, Cuy-a-ho-ga Coun-ty, O-hi-o, there was born a babe, whose name was des-tined to be up-on the lips of all the civ-il-ized world. This was James A-bram Gar-field, our mur-dered Pres-i-dent.

His fath-er, A-bram Gar-field, was mar-ried in 1819, to E-li-za Bal-lou, a daugh-ter of the Rhode Is-land fam-i-ly of that name. When her hus-band died in 1833, leav-ing Mrs. Gar-field, whose life had most-ly been spent in the wild West, with four chil-dren to care for, and lit-tle or no mo-ney to do it with, she put all her pow-ers

to work to bring them up as they should be.   Ear-ly
and late she toiled for them; and James, see-ing her
strug-gle, made up his mind that he would help her
as soon as he was large e-nough.   While still a
small boy, he took the place of driv-er on a ca-nal
boat called "E-ven-ing Star," but a se-vere at-tack of
ague made him give up this place.   He went to the
dis-trict school, and by the time he was eigh-teen
had learned all he could in it.

In 1851 he en-tered the "Ec-lec-tic In-sti-tute,"
now Hi-ram Col-lege, at Hi-ram, O-hi-o, where he
fit-ted for col-lege.   It was a word from the Pres-i-
dent—Mark Hop-kins—which led James A. Gar-
field to choose Wil-liams Col-lege, at Wil-liams-
town, Mass-a-chu-setts, from which he grad-u-at-ed
with the high-est hon-ors of his class, in 1856.

In 1858 he mar-ried Lu-cre-tia Ru-dolph, the
grand-niece of a duke.   When the war came he
went to the front as Lieu-ten-ant-Col-o-nel of the 42d
O-hi-o Vo-lun-teers, and was made Brig-a-dier-Gen-
er-al on Jan-u-a-ry 10, 1862.   Gen-er-al Gar-field
was a Com-man-der at Shi-loh, was called to be
Chief of Staff by Gen-er-al Rose-crans, and was with
George H. Thom-as at the aw-ful fight at Chick-a-
mau-ga.   For his brave deeds at that bat-tle he was
made a Ma-jor-Gen-er-al.

Dur-ing the sec-ond year of the war, his friends

in O-hi-o chose him to go to Con-gress; and by the ad-vice of Pres-i-dent Lin-coln and Gen-er-al Rose-crans, he de-cid-ed to go, and took his seat—the young-est mem-ber of Con-gress—on De-cem-ber 5, 1863, giv-ing up his place in the ar-my the same day. To this bod-y he was nine times e-lect-ed.

In Jan-u-a-ry of 1880 he was chos-en by the State of O-hi-o to the Sen-ate, for the six years end-ing March 4, 1887; but on June 10, 1880, he was nom-in-at-ed for Pres-i-dent.

On March 4, 1881, he was in-aug-u-rat-ed; and on Ju-ly 2nd he was shot by a cow-ard-ly as-sas-sin. Ev-er-y-thing was done to save his life, but to no pur-

THE SQUARE, CLEVE-LAND.

pose, for on Sep-tem-ber 19th, at El-be-ron, New Jer-sey, he died, sad-ly mourned for by the whole world.

His bod-y was ta-ken to Cleve-land, and laid to rest in Lake View Cem-e-te-ry, one of the most beau-ti-ful cem-e-ter-ies in the coun-try.

Pres-i-dent Gar-field loved this fair ci-ty of the
North, with its beau-ti-ful square, and fin-est streets
in our land ; and his rest-ing-place on the shore of
Lake E-rie would no doubt have been his wish, had
he had a voice in the mat-ter.

CHAPTER XXXVII.

NEWSPAPERS AND NEWSPAPER MEN.

THOSE of my young friends who have been in
Cin-cin-na-ti must have no-ticed the fine build-ing on
the cor-ner of Vine and Sixth streets, which has
been for ma-ny years the home of the *Ga-zette*, one
of the old-est and strong-est of West-ern news-pa-
pers.   For o-ver sev-en-ty and five years it has been
read by O-hi-o peo-ple, while its own-er, Mr. Rich-
ard Smith, is one of the best known and most pub-lic
spir-it-ed men in Cin-cin-na-ti.   A few years a-go
the pa-per was merged in the *Com-mer-cial*, which
now stands first in the State, and is well known all
o-ver the Un-ion.

The Cin-cin-na-ti *Com-mer-cial* was first print-ed
in 1843 by Messrs. Cur-tis and Has-tings.   For
ma-ny years the name of Mu-rat Hal-stead at its
head has made it fa-mous all o-ver our land.   Mr.

Hal-stead is one of the bright-est of men, and the
keen, wit-ty things which come from his pen are
cop-ied and talked a-bout by pa-pers in all parts
of our coun-try.

The *En-quir-er* is a pa-per ev-er-y-one reads.
Some years a-go Mr. John R. Mc-Lean
was made its ed-i-tor, and he has made it
the pleas-ant sheet we
all love to read.

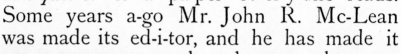

The *Volks-blatt*, the
lead-ing Ger-man pa-per
in the State, owes its
high place to the a-ble
and pains-tak-ing ed-i-
tor, Mr. F.
Has-sau-rek,
who stood at its
head for ma-ny
years. Mr.
Has-sau-rek,
though born in
Vi-en-na, came

SCENES ON THE O-HI-O.

to A-mer-i-ca and set-tled at Cin-cin-na-ti in 1848.
This is why we claim him as an O-hi-o man.

Dur-ing the war he was sent to South A-mer-i-ca
as U-nit-ed States Min-is-ter to E-qua-dor. In
1865 he start-ed the *Volks-blatt*. He died in Par-is

RIV-ER FRONT OF CIN-CIN-NA-TI.

on the 3d of Oc-to-ber, 1885, leav-ing ma-ny to mourn for him both in this coun-try and the Old World.

The *Sat-ur-day Night* is the "fun-ny" pa-per of Cin-cin-na-ti, and in it Mi-nor.Gris-wold, "The Fat Con-trib-u-tor," makes fun for old and young. The *Times-Star* is one of the bright pa-pers read in the e-ven-ing by the folks of Cin-cin-na-ti.

In Co-lum-bus four pa-pers are print-ed each day, and a num-ber are sent forth once a week, while oth-ers still come to us but once a month.

In 1811, Col-o-nel James Kil-bourne start-ed a pa-per in the lit-tle town of Worth-ing-ton, some ten miles from "High Bank on the Sci-o-to." This he called the *West-ern In-tel-li-gen-cer.* Three years la-ter he moved his of-fice to Co-lum-bus, where it has been ev-er since; on-ly the name of the pa-per was changed in 1825 to the *O-hi-o State Jour-nal,* a name it still bears.

One of its ed-i-tors was Gov-er-nor John Grei-ner, fa-mous for his songs, which were sung in all parts of our land during the cam-paign when Pres-i-dent Har-ri-son was e-lect-ed to his of-fice. Gen-er-al Wil-liam Schou-ler was its ed-i-tor just be-fore, and Dr. I-saac J. Al-len dur-ing, the war.

At one time Wil-liam Dean How-ells, one of the most not-ed au-thors O-hi-o has ev-er giv-en to us,

ON THE SCI-O-TO.

was at its head. Mr. How-ells was born in this State, and spent his ear-ly life here. His fa-ther was the ed-i-tor of a coun-try pa-per, and a care-ful stu-dent; so the boy How-ells was

ON THE FARM.

brought up with plen-ty of good books in his home, and the free, hap-py life on an O-hi-o farm to give him strength and vig-or of bod-y as well as mind. While still a lad he learned to set type, and while in the of-fice he of-ten wrote po-ems for the

pa-per on which he worked. His first book was
called " Po-ems by Two Friends," and was made up
of his own po-ems and those of his friend, A. San-
ders Pi-att.

Mr. How-ells is now on the ed-i-tor-i-al staff of
Har-per's Mag-a-zine. He has for ma-ny years
writ-ten for our best mag-a-zines, and his sto-ries are
ea-ger-ly looked for by thou-sands of read-ers, both
here and on the oth-er side of the sea.

The *Dai-ly Times* is an-oth-er morn-ing pa-per,
while the *Dis-patch* reach-es us at night-fall. The
Ger-man *West-bote* is al-so an a-ble Co-lum-bus
pa-per.

CHAPTER XXXVIII.

SOME PUBLIC MEN AND THEIR WORKS.

Pos-si-bly no State in our Un-ion has more
pub-lic spir-it-ed men and wo-men than O-hi-o. By
pub-lic spir-it-ed I mean those who by their works or
their gold try to make the world bet-ter or wis-er.

Of these, Mrs. Bel-la-my Stor-er, of Cin-cin-na-ti,
whose love for true art and the beau-ti-ful has led
her to main-tain the Rook-wood pot-ter-y with her
own gold, is one of the lead-ing spir-its. Those

whose names are con-nect-ed with the found-ing of the Mu-se-um and the Art School should al-ways be thought of with love by ev-er-y O-hi-o boy and girl. Of these Mr. Nich-o-las Long-worth, Mr. R. R. Spring-er, Mr. Charles R. West, and Mr. Da-vid Sin-ton, are the best known.

The Col-lege of Mu-sic, which owes its be-ing more to Mr. R. R. Spring-er than to an-y oth-er per-son, is one of the best mu-si-cal schools in the coun-try; while its great hall, with its walls and ceil-ing of wood, is one of the best con-cert halls in the world.

Mr. A. W. Whelp-ley, the li-bra-ri-an of the Free Pub-lic Li-bra-ry, is a true work-er for the pub-lic good ; for by his cul-ti-vat-ed taste, he guides and forms that of ma-ny of the young read-ers of Cin-cin-na-ti.

Though born in New York, Wil-liam Slo-comb Groes-beck has lived in Cin-cin-na-ti for so ma-ny years that he is claimed by that ci-ty as a part of it-self. Mr. Groes-beck is one of the bright-est men in O-hi-o, and has for ma-ny years held high pla-ces of trust in the gov-ern-ment of both State and coun-try.

To-le-do, too, has her share of great men. Of these Frank Hunt Hurd, who was born at Mount Ver-non, O-hi-o, on Christ-mas Day, 1841, is the best known. Mr. Hurd grad-u-at-ed at Ken-yon Col-lege, a-bout thir-ty years a-go, and since that time he has held some of the high-est of-fi-ces in the land. He has ev-er been a friend to the best in-ter-ests of our coun-try, and has al-ways had the cour-age

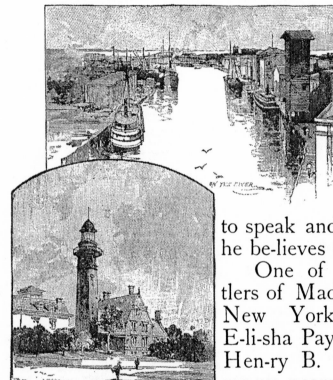

THE RIV-ER AND LIGHT-HOUSE AT CLEVE-LAND.

to speak and to write what he be-lieves to be right.

One of the ear-ly set-tlers of Mad-i-son Coun-ty, New York, was Judge E-li-sha Payne, whose son, Hen-ry B. Payne, has for ma-ny years been claimed as a Cleve-land man. Though Mr. Payne was born in New York State, he came to Cleve-land when a young man, and prac-tised law in that place. Since that time he has ev-er been one of the most not-ed men in north-ern O-hi-o, hav-ing been sent to Con-gress, and called up-on to serve the State in some of her high-est of-fi-ces.

A few years be-fore the war there came to Cleve-land a poor, foot-sore, and rag-ged young man, who had walked most of the way from his home in Maine in hopes of get-ting a place in some news-pa-per of-fice in our fair ci-ty of the North. When he called at the of-fice of the *Cleve-land Plain-deal-er,* he looked much more like a tramp than a writ-er; but the clear-head-ed ed-i-tor of that pa-per, with an in-sight, born, per-haps, from his kind-ness of heart, took the poor fel-low in, and in time was re-paid ten-fold for this act.

Charles H. Browne—or "Ar-te-mus Ward," as he called him-self in print—soon be-came known all through our land, and his fun-ny say-ings were cop-ied by pa-pers ev-er-y-where. It is said that Pres-i-dent Lin-coln was ver-y fond of his wit, and used to keep *Ar-te-mus Ward, His Book,* which was filled with bits of Browne's fun-ny tales, on his desk; so that when tired and worn by the heav-y cares which weighed up-on him, he could rest his mind and clear his thoughts by read-ing a few pa-ges of the fun-ny man's wit and non-sense.

Mr. Browne died in Eng-land some twen-ty years a-go, while the guest of the son of the fa-mous po-et, Thom-as Hood.

Cleve-land may well be proud to claim as a son Col-o-nel John Hay, who has for ma-ny years lived with-in her lim-its. Though born in Il-li-nois, Col-o-nel Hay is al-ways looked up-on as an O-hi-o man. He was born in 1839, and in the course of time grad-u-at-ed from Brown U-ni-ver-si-ty, Prov-i-dence. Af-ter this he wrote for pa-pers and books. His sketch-es of rough life on the Miss-is-sip-pi are viv-id word pic-tures of the folk who lived on its banks be-fore the war. Just now his name is known all o-ver the world as one of the au-thors of the " His-to-ry of A-bra-ham Lin-coln," which comes to us each month through the pa-ges of the *Cen-tu-ry Mag-a-zine.*

Xe-ni-a, too, has a son in whom not on-ly she, but the whole land, takes a just pride. This is White-law Read, the world-re-nowned ed-i-tor of the *New York Trib-une.* Though New York would glad-ly call him hers, it was in Xe-ni-a his ba-by eyes first o-pened to the light, and so she has a pri-or claim to his fame. As you know, ev-er-y ci-ty and town lays a claim to, and in fact seems to think it has in some way helped to make the fame of, its great men.

Al-len G. Thur-man, whom ma-ny men in our land hope to have for our next Vice-Pres-i-dent, though born in Lynch-burg, Vir-gin-ia, came to live in O-hi-o when he was but six years old. His fath-er, who was a Bap-tist min-is-ter, did not think it right to keep slaves, and said so. When he had freed his own, he found the folk near his home were no long-er friends to him, and so he moved a-cross the O-hi-o Riv-er and set-tled in Chil-li-coth-e. His son Al-len was sent to school, and was soon found to be the bright-est boy in the place. At that time a French em-i-grant came to the town, and young Thur-man learned his first French from him. In time he be-came a fine French schol-ar. La-ter he stud-ied law. Mr. Thur-man now lives in a large house in Co-lum-bus, with his son and four small grand-chil-dren, who are a great com-fort to the kind-ly old man.

AL-LEN G. THUR-MAN.

While in the Sen-ate of the U-nit-ed States, Mr. Thur-man was not-ed for a won-der-ful snuff-box and a red silk ban-dan-na hand-ker-chief; and it was the lat-ter that led his friends to choose for his em-blem the "ban-dan-na," which just now is seen wav-ing in all parts of our land.

O-hi-o is in-deed rich in brave and wise men, and it would take a book ma-ny times the size of this to tell of them all. But if through these pa-ges

a love for the his-to-ry of the State, and that of her
hon-ored sons and daugh-ters, has been formed, it
will be an ea-sy mat-ter to go on with the stud-y ; for
in books made for old-er folk you will find much
which tells of both plac-es and men that will more
than re-pay you for the hard work you may have in
try-ing to read them.

CHAPTER XXXIX.

NATURE'S GIFTS TO OHIO.

WHAT do you think the In-dians, or e-ven the
white men who first came to our State, would say, if
they could for a few hours wake from their long
sleep and look up-on the great gas-fields which stretch
o-ver vast a-re-as in O-hi-o. They did not know of
coal e-ven ; and the woods which came close to their
doors gave them no chance to dread the time when
fu-el would be scarce.

A hun-dred years have not yet passed, but most
of the great trees which could be spared have been
felled and used; some for fires, and oth-ers for
hous-es, or in mak-ing the ta-bles, chairs, and bed-
steads which go to fit up our homes.

So it is that for years past men have been forced

to use oth-er fu-el than wood to feed the great fires which keep our vast man-u-fac-to-ries at work, and Na-ture—who, by the way, seems to smile more kind-ly up-on O-hi-o than up-on ma-ny oth-er parts of our land—has giv-en us first coal and then nat-ur-al gas for this.

The coal was a no-ble gift; for through it we have be-come one of the rich-est States in the Un-ion. Still, the great cloud of smoke which has for years dimmed our sky and made our hous-es din-gy and black has nev-er been liked by our peo-ple, who were forced to use the soft coal which caused it. So it is with joy in-deed that the gas is greet-ed, for it does a-way with all the dirt and smoke; and a-gain the fair O-hi-o sky has a chance to smile o-ver her cit-ies and towns as it used to do in the days of long a-go. In fact the whole land seems changed by this new gift.

So you see that though O-hi-o was a wil-der-ness filled with In-dians, and scarce-ly dreamed of by the white men when the At-lan-tic States were well sprin-kled o-ver with church-es and schools, we have made such rap-id strides that we have not on-ly caught up with our sis-ter States, but in some things have out-stripped them in the race.

E-ven Na-ture is par-tial to O-hi-o; and it would be strange in-deed if her sons and daugh-ters were

not proud of this "land which gave them birth."
When they re-mem-ber that through their veins
there cours-es the best of New Eng-land blood, min-
gled, per-haps, with that of the a-ris-to-crats of old
Vir-gin-ia, they may well be proud and glad of the
kind fate which has giv-en them this roy-al her-i-
tage.

The boys and girls of to-day will, in a few years,
be the men and wo-men of our State; and as O-hi-o
has been rich in fa-mous per-sons in the past, you
must re-mem-ber, my dear young friends, that it
rests with you to keep up her fair rep-u-ta-tion.
God for-bid that so ma-ny brave sol-diers may ev-er
a-gain be need-ed in our land, but there are oth-er
ways in which you may shed glo-ry on the dear home
State.   Mu-si-cians and paint-ers, men of let-ters—
of which we have al-read-y a good-ly num-ber—and
schol-ars in all the sci-en-ces are ev-er need-ed in this
wide world of ours.   In these and ma-ny oth-er ways
you may help to swell the his-to-ry of O-hi-o, which
will ev-er go on as long as the U-nit-ed States of
A-mer-i-ca con-tin-ue to ex-ist.

THE END.

Printed in the United States
33329LVS00003B/50